D0777288

Clouded Dreams |

Clouded Dreams

Deborah Insel

DELPHINIUM BOOKS

Harrison, New York   **Encino, California**

Excerpts from PEARL'S KITCHEN, AN EXTRAORDINARY COOKBOOK, copyright © 1973 by Pearl Bailey, reprinted by permission of Harcourt Brace & Company.

Jacket photograph © David Burch, Shooting Back, Inc., 1989

Library of Congress Cataloging-in-Publication Data
Insel, Deborah, 1949-
    Clouded Dreams / by Deborah Insel, — 1st ed.
       p. cm
    ISBN 1-883285-04-6 : $19.95
    I. Title
PS3559.N75C57 1995
813'.54—dc20

Published by Delphinium Books, Inc.
P.O. Box 703
Harrison, New York 10528

Distributed by Publishers Group West
Printed in the United States of America
Jacket and text design by Neuwirth & Associates, Inc.

For Robert Silber, Dad, who always believed in me

What greater or better gift can we offer the Republic than to teach and instruct our youth?

—*Cicero*

Justitia Omnibus—Justice for all.

—Official motto of the District of Columbia

Be ashamed to die until you have won some victory for humanity.

—*Horace Mann*

Hungry people cannot be good at learning or producing anything except perhaps violence.

—*Pearl Bailey*

Clouded Dreams |

Cirri

CIRRI FELT MARCUS TURN OVER in bed and run a hand up her thigh. Though she saw gray under the window shade, she was warm and tired and didn't want to be awake yet. She ignored him. Mama would be home soon, she knew, and here they were in Mama's bed. In a way, Cirri didn't care. Mama was gone every night, left Cirri in charge of her younger brother and sister. Why shouldn't she be able to have her boyfriend spend the night if she wanted to? Having him there made things easier. Only, Mama would be upset if she knew. That was the problem.

Marcus didn't move for a few minutes. Then he slid his hand to her stomach, down across her private area to her thigh again.

Better to get Marcus up and out of the house before Mama came home. "You had enough of my little ass last night," she warned. "You don't get no more this morning."

He chuckled. "You're a tough one, Cirri James."

"Uh huh."

He nudged her neck with his nose and kissed her under her chin. "Sweet, though."

"They's grape jelly in the kitchen. You don't be needing me for sweet."

"You need me, though," he whispered into her neck.

"Like a fool needs a dunce cap."

He pressed himself against her. "Why're you like this this morning?"

"Because I gotta get up and I don't want to."

"So you're mad at me? What kind of sense does that make?"

She studied the set of his jaw and the fine muscle standing out on his neck. His arms were crossed behind his head. And she was almost taken in by him. She was tempted just to nestle her head in under his chin again. But she knew better than to get comfortable. There was too much else to do and to worry about.

She flung back the blanket and stood, pulled on a sweatshirt and jeans. "Who said anything about sense? I just gotta get up. And you should too."

He stretched his arms. "Yeah. I gotta get to school."

She jammed a hand onto her hip. "You're going right on back there?"

"That's right."

"Well, I guess you better go because if you're that dumb, then you do need some schooling."

He laughed. "Come on with me, Cirri."

She threw his jeans at him and stalked out of the bedroom.

"Well, what you gonna do all day?" he shouted after her.

"I'm gonna go shopping and maybe watch me some TV."

She shook the little boy on one end of the couch. "Get up,

Willie." Then she went to the other end and stroked the girl's head. "Pea. It's time."

"Mama home?" Pea asked.

Cirri stood up. "No. Get stirring." She went to the kitchen. "You don't need Mama anyway. You got your Cirri here."

With the refrigerator door open, she stood and contemplated the inside. There was some Kentucky Fried Chicken left over from last night, halves of two chocolate milk shakes, grape jelly and four loaves of white bread. She arranged the three chicken pieces in a pie pan and put them in the oven. Then she made jelly sandwiches and wrapped them carefully in waxed paper.

Marcus ambled into the kitchen rubbing his neck.

"They gonna need milk money," she said.

He dug into his pants pocket. "How much is it?"

She skirted him and shouted around the corner. "Pea, hey, I tole you to get up. Now come on. Willie!"

His buying them supper last night was one thing. She knew, then, she was going to be giving him a kind of payback later on in the bed. But this morning asking him for even fifty cents seemed like too much. She wouldn't have done it except that the kids needed it.

"Quarter each," she mumbled when she came back.

He put it on the counter beside the sandwiches.

"I'm making you some breakfast," she said to him, trying to get the money out of her mind.

He looked in the oven and shook his head. "Chicken?"

"A hot, healthy breakfast."

He sat at the table and stretched his long legs. "If you aren't going to school, why don't you get a job?"

She busied herself washing glasses. She didn't like him asking questions, especially questions she couldn't answer. She didn't want him knowing too much about her life. There were only a few solid things that she knew for sure, and she felt she should hoard these. "I'm thinking about it."

"And?"

"And, I don't know. Some days I think I'll go to school. Get me my high school diploma. And some days, I think I won't." She shouted at Willie as he was on his way to the bathroom. "Wash the sleep out your eyes and hurry up. Pea, I mean it. Right now."

Pea shaded her eyes against the light in the kitchen and sat down at the table. Cirri measured out equal portions of the two milk shakes into three glasses. She lifted chicken onto three plates and put them on the table.

"Don't you have another shirt?" she asked Pea. "That one's dirty on the sleeves and wrinkled up besides."

"No."

Cirri grumbled, "Okay, I'll wash today."

Willie came in and sat down to his food.

"Aren't you eating?" Marcus asked Cirri quietly.

"Ain't hungry now."

"Come on. You can have some of this."

She shook her head.

"If you come to school I'll buy you a nice lunch at C & J's."

"I got washing to do."

He held out his arms and shimmied his shoulders. "Don't you want to see me strut back into that school?"

"You'll have an audience whether I'm there or not."

"Think Jasper'll be surprised to see me?"

"No. He knows you'll come back since you got business to conduct at that school. And if you go back, you're stupid 'cause he'll catch you and throw you out for good."

"It's my business that fed you last night," Marcus loudly reminded her.

She glanced at Willie and Pea then at the floor, embarrassed. "I know that."

"So?"

"I wish I didn't have to take your money."

"Baby, I don't mind," he said.

"But I mind how you get it."

"I'm nothing and you know it. Small little cog in a big ol' machine."

"Big enough for Jasper to notice."

"He couldn't prove nothing and you know it."

"But he will next time. Then where will you be?"

He grinned. "Your lunch ticket be gone."

"You'll be at Oak Hill or Lorton," she yelled. "And I don't want you there."

"Why not?" he asked soberly.

"You two finish up," she said to the kids, hoping Marcus would leave too, before Mama came. "That school bus gonna be here."

She met his gaze.

"Why not?" he repeated.

She grabbed the sandwiches and quarters and jammed them into the children's pockets. "Because I care about you. All right? That's why," she said.

He slung his arm around her waist and smiled. "I thought you did."

She searched his face for any hint that he cared about her, too. But all she saw was his wide, carefree grin and the skin crimped at the side of his eyes that made him look so sincere, so appealing. A dozen girls at school would love to be in this kitchen now, waking up with him, and he knew it. She didn't know why he'd chosen her.

She edged away from him, grabbed the chicken on Willie's plate and pulled off pieces of the meat. "Eat that or you're gonna be hungry." Pea had finished her food. Cirri took her away from the table and dragged the brush through her hair, fixed it with two rubber bands, then held the jacket for the girl. "Willie, you ready?"

There was a fumbling at the lock on the front door. Cirri, knowing it was Mama, knowing there was going to be trouble now, dropped the jacket as Pea ran to the door and opened it.

"Mama!" the little girl screamed.

Willie, being older, understanding more, hung back.

Mama bent over Pea and they hugged each other. Then Mama stood up and held out two loaves of white bread to Cirri. "Here, put these away."

Cirri took them without a word and threw them onto the table.

"Think you're too big of a man to gimme a hug?" Mama asked Willie.

Her head wobbled on her neck like the dolls' heads on springs in the back of cars. Her coat had a long, dark stain down the front. She wore dirty aqua bedroom slippers.

Willie approached her and silently accepted her groping hug. Then she patted his back. "Okay. Now go to school." She looked up at the ceiling and tried to catch her breath. "All three a' you. Go on, get outta here to school."

When her eyes finally landed on Marcus, she narrowed them and tilted backward till Cirri thought she would fall. Then she righted herself again. Marcus leaned in the bedroom doorway and watched her.

"You got a boy in here, Cirri?" she screamed. She pushed past Marcus in a sudden rush and stared at the bed. "You fucking this boy in my bed?"

Cirri herded the kids out the front door. "Go on," she said.

Then she closed the door and rested her head against it. Mama whirled around the room, waving her arms, the sides of her coat flying like great dusty bird wings. "Fucking this boy right here. And he has the audacity to keep on staring at me and not even leave out this house. And you fucking in front of these children. I should throw you out. Those babies that don't know nothing about this world and you're bringing boys in here . . . and in my bed. All that scum on my sheets!"

Cirri glanced at Marcus. He seemed cool and calm as ever, not mad, not worried. Maybe his house was like this, too. She didn't know anything about his family.

Mama was embarrassing Cirri. She wasn't usually so loud; she hardly ever got mad like this. But Cirri knew that she'd done things with Marcus last night that they shouldn't have done, things she'd regret, so she probably deserved this from Mama. Still, it made her nervous for Marcus to be seeing it.

Cirri glared at him. "Ain't you going to school?"

"Miss the fun here?" He smiled crookedly.

"What fun?" Mama demanded. "Ain't you had your fun? How dare you stay here a minute longer? I got to get this house in order!" Then she strayed off again toward the couch, ranting to herself.

"That's what your 'business' does to people," Cirri spat. She didn't want to be mad at Marcus. She wanted his reassurance, but she couldn't help herself.

"I didn't sell it to her," Marcus returned, coming over to Cirri.

"Might as well have."

"She in the big leagues. Bad enough already," he said, turning to watch her again.

"That's right!" Cirri said.

He turned back around. "I don't want to ever see you on none of that stuff."

She thrust her hands onto her hips. "Oh. You selling it, but you don't want to see nobody on it. How you explain that?"

"Just making a little money," he said and put his hand on the doorknob. "If you come to school you don't have to face her."

Cirri thought there was some kindness in his voice, some desire to save her the pain she was going through. But probably not. Probably he just wanted her at school for his own reasons.

She shook her head. He kissed her temple and opened the door.

"I bring home good food into this house," Mama was shouting, swaying back toward Cirri. "This home, this good home, for my children."

"Two loaves of bread?" Cirri waved them at her. "We already got four goddamned loaves in there. What we need bread for? What about milk for those children? Huh? What about hamburg?"

She heard the door click shut behind her and she wanted to cry.

"What happened to our food stamps for this month?" Cirri continued. "Our AFDC check? They gone, ain't they? Shot up. Gone up in smoke. Ain't that right? And what we gonna do now?"

Later, Cirri used the bar of soap to scrub clothes in the bathroom sink. She wrung out the gray water and hung Pea's and Willie's jeans on the towel rack. The shower rod was broken, so Cirri stretched underwear and two shirts across the backs of the kitchen chairs. Then she washed herself a bra, some socks and her favorite sweater. She washed a blouse for Mama and her brown corduroy jeans. She hoped Mama'd wear the pants instead of those flimsy dresses, now that the weather was cold.

Mama was sleeping on the bed, still in her coat, one arm

flung out like she was reaching for something. She had calmed down after Marcus left. With him gone, she had seemed to forget that he had ever been there. She had held her head and complained of being tired. Cirri had helped her into bed. Nothing would wake Mama at this stage, Cirri knew from experience. So she felt in the pockets of the coat. Thirty-seven cents and a half pack of cigarettes. She hunted in the dress pockets, the bra. There was a dollar tucked in there.

She slipped the money into her jeans. Mama wouldn't miss it. She didn't even know she had it. Cirri pulled the blanket up over Mama, bent the one arm in so it wouldn't get cold, and left the apartment.

Once down the metal stairs, she checked Furry's apartment. There was no reason for her to look in at it every time she passed, but she always did, maybe just to marvel at the damage fire could do, to wonder if anyone was fixing it up yet, to see if Furry had come back. Furry always had a joke for her and the kids. Sometimes he gave them quarters for ice cream. He used to look out for them. But then he started having trouble with the hustlers. He owed them a lot of money. So they burned this place. And he'd been gone a long time now.

It wasn't a big fire. Still, the firemen had broken the windows getting to it, and the wall where the couch was—where they'd lit the papers—was charred and cracked. Smoke had made the ceiling and all the other walls sooty. Water had ruined the rug. The front door was left open—there wasn't anything to steal. People had been dumping their trash in there. It smelled of rotten garbage and pee.

She noticed a small movement in one corner and she stepped back, poised to run if it was a rat. But a little yellow kitten emerged from the trash, tiptoed over the papers, and rubbed itself against her leg. When she petted it, it meowed. It was skinny and its eyes were runny. "Poor little thing," she murmured. Her hands, dry and ashy from the washing, stung when they brushed against the kitten's fur.

Cirri pushed through the battered metal doors of the building and out into the sunlight. She squinted against the sun flashing off the pavement, struck out across the basketball court toward the McDonald's.

"Hey, baby," the pusher on the corner said. "You lookin' nice. Wanna feel nice, too?"

She kept her pace, hands down in her pockets, seeing her breath blow back in her face.

"Good rocks, here, honey. What? You too fine to buy?" called another pusher from a doorway.

She knew they were harmless. Just walk by. They didn't bother her.

What bothered her was to think Marcus was one of them, only he did it over by the school. He stood under a tree six steps from the gym door and spoke low to kids like this when they walked by, kept the stuff in a paper bag jammed up in a crotch in the tree. A little work at lunchtime and he made thirty, forty dollars a day. He said he wasn't going for the big time—that came with big-time problems—he just wanted to make some steady money. He had regular customers at school. It was simple. Only thing was, Dr. Jasper knew. He had suspended Marcus, given him fair warning, he said. Next time Marcus would be selling to an agent, the principal had said.

Cirri stalked on. Her sweatshirt wasn't anything against this cold. Her ears were numb. But she didn't have far to go.

She pictured him at school. Where would he be now? On the way to Miz Brown's class. "Back in school after a three-day vacation," he'd be saying. "Played a little basketball, caught up on my soaps, took it nice and easy." He wouldn't mention Cirri. That much she knew. If she were there, he would fling his arm over her shoulder and say they'd spent some time together. But since she wasn't, the other girls could crowd around and listen and jive back to him.

"Miz Brown been missing you, Marcus," Dione would say. "Ain't got no one to pick on with me gone, do she?"

"We gonna get her lecture on ghetto economics again, for sure, thanks to you," Akeesha would complain.

And Marcus would pinch her cheek and grin. "I know you looking forward to catching up on your sleep. Well, you go ahead. Let her pick on me till all the nits are gone. And you have yourself a nice little nap."

If she were there, she could protect her claim to him. But out here, she was just a memory. She wasn't sure why she didn't just go on to school with him like he'd asked. His showing off wouldn't really bother her. He had to do that—everybody did when they came back from suspension—had to show that Jasper wasn't nothing.

She would have enjoyed it, actually, because with his arm hanging across her shoulders, his hand dangling by her breast, there would be no doubt about them. People would look at her in a different way, walking with Marcus Chance. Some of his glory would rub off on her. People liked him. He was generous with his money, which was probably why he stood out to Jasper in the first place.

She couldn't figure out why she acted so short with him this morning except that she was nervous about Mama coming home. Still, that wasn't enough reason to be so irritated when she didn't want to be. It was like she was trying to get rid of him when just the opposite was true.

She took her hands out of her pockets and crossed her arms against a blast of cold wind when she turned the corner. Then she hurried into McDonald's. The smell of the eggs and sausage and coffee made her stomach rumble. She got in line behind a couple of three-piece-suiters and studied the people behind the counter. They were pushing the words on the cash register, hurrying to grab the wrapped and boxed food, pouring coffee, accepting twenty-dollar bills, making change.

The three-piece-suiters, busy talking about some case of this or that, picked up their loaded trays and walked past her to a table. It was in this city, just a few blocks away, that the government was run. That's what they were told often enough in school, ever since kindergarten. "In this very city, Washington, D.C., decisions are made every minute that affect the country and the whole world. You live in the seat of power." It was supposed to make them feel important. It didn't work, though. The government was too far away.

Cirri moved to the front of the line and asked the man at the cash register for an application form.

"You're not ordering anything?" he asked.

"No."

"Okay, go wait over there till I finish with these customers."

At least it was warm inside. She sat down at a table and watched people eat. Saliva flooded her mouth and her stomach growled. She looked out the window. Down the street were the big office buildings where the suits came from.

She had once had a plan to become a secretary in one of those buildings after she graduated from Grant. Mama had been a secretary at the Interior Department, and she'd enjoyed the work—answering the phone, taking messages, typing letters, copying and collating papers, keeping the office organized. Cirri had thought she could easily work during the days, go to school nights. She had figured it would take her a long time doing it that way, but she wanted to be a doctor, a doctor for kids. There was a way about little kids when they were sick that affected her. She'd seen it in Pea and Willie. They might be throwing up or burning with a fever, but they didn't make a big deal out of it the way adults did. Maybe that was because they didn't know what was happening to them; they didn't know enough to worry. They were brave and generally happy even when they were feeling miserable. They were grateful for what anyone did for them. And when they started feeling better, they jumped up and started running around like nothing had ever happened.

The motto over the door to the library at school was in her head. *If you can imagine it, you can achieve it. If you can dream it, you can become it.* She could see herself as a pediatrician. But already her plan was bogged down, and her goal seemed as far away as the clouds. Other things were getting in the way.

She was taking typing at school But she hadn't been to school enough and now the class was way ahead of her, too far for her to catch up. She knew she had to have that typing in order to get an office job.

And here she was at McDonald's. If she took a job here, she would never have time to get back to school. But the present was more pressing than the future. What if she didn't have what it took to be a kid doctor anyway? That was a faraway, shadowy idea. Mama sick and the kids needing her was real.

On the opposite end of the street was a woman poking an umbrella at something on the sidewalk. At first, from the way she walked, Cirri thought it was Mama. But she knew Mama would be asleep a long time yet. The woman looked like a mental, and Cirri was glad she was inside. The street crazies scared her more than the hustlers.

She wondered if Mama looked like a mental to other people. In that filthy coat and bedroom slippers, probably so. Cirri didn't know where Mama went almost every night. She was scared to find out, didn't want to know, didn't want to know anything about it.

Finally, the man brought her the application. "We don't

have any openings right now," he said. "But we do have them once in a while. I'll keep this on file and give you a call."

Cirri nodded. There was no phone at home. She figured she would stop in every week or so to check. He lent her an ink pen, and she filled out everything she could. Under experience, she wrote, *I make good hamburgers.* But a friend had told her that at McDonald's everything was automatic, all done by machines. There wasn't any real cooking. Her answer seemed silly, so she crossed it out. When she handed him back the paper, he slid it onto the counter next to some spilled orange juice and didn't say another word to her.

Back out on the sidewalk, she felt a littler warmer, but hungrier. She half jogged the three blocks to her friend Thea's house.

Thea's six-month-old son, Bryan, was perched on Thea's hip. His nose was runny and tears clung to his cheeks. Drool ran down onto his sleeper.

"Come on in," Thea said. "First time he's stopped crying all morning."

Cirri was taken, as she always was, with the baby's balloon cheeks and wide-set eyes. She held out her hands to him. "That's 'cause he just been waiting for some hot number to come play with him. Ain't that right, Bryan?"

"Well, good, you two have a ball," Thea said and walked away toward the TV. "He kept me up half the night with his snifflin' and fussin'."

The house was dark and smelled of dirty diapers, but it was warm and Cirri felt comfortable in it. She and Thea had been friends a long time. She knew this house like she knew her own. There was considerably more furniture here, more knickknacks, newspapers, cozy clutter. Thea's mom had thrown rugs over the threadbare spots in the orange carpet, and the plastic flower arrangement on the TV was dusty but cheerful. There was a homeyness here that she missed in her own place. Cirri, carrying Bryan, went to the kitchen, took a napkin from the holder on the table, and wiped his nose and cheeks. He started to fuss.

"See, I told you," Thea yelled. "Maybe you ain't such a hot ticket after all."

Cirri came back to the front room and sat down in one of the big chairs facing the TV. Thea was heavy under her pink nightgown, still big in the hips and bust from the pregnancy. Her hair was standing out every which way. Cirri hadn't meant to hurt her feelings with the comment about being a hot ticket. She knew Thea was sensitive about her weight now.

She bounced Bryan on her knees and distracted him from his crying. Thea was absorbed in the game show.

"Marcus went back to school today," Cirri said.

"Marcus think he too cool to get busted, but he gonna come up short one day. One way or another."

"I told him."

Bryan's nose was running again but she didn't want to wipe it for fear he would cry. He was happy to be bounced.

Thea and her family were fierce about drugs. So much so that Thea had endured a "very difficult" childbirth, as the doctor called it, without anesthetic of any kind. Cirri had heard Thea's father say many times, "For the Indians, it's alcohol. For the black man, it's cocaine and heroin. It's a weakness in our systems. But if you don't have that first taste, you don't get caught." Thea said it had felt like hot knives when they cut her down below to get Bryan out, but she was afraid to ask for any drugs.

Thea's father was a government courier, driving documents back and forth between buildings. He had even been in the White House on delivery. Thea's mother worked in the cafeteria of the Air and Space Museum. They had been angry when Thea got pregnant. But at least, they had said, "She ain't done nothing illegal, and she ain't messed up her mind."

Cirri felt comfortable here in this house, knowing where things were, knowing she was welcomed. At the same time she felt uncomfortable because she could never talk about what went on at her house.

"And to think I once loved Marcus Chance like he was a living god," Thea said, not looking away from the screen. "Um. Um. Um."

Bryan's drool was sliding down Cirri's hand, but his face, jiggling like Jell-O, was gleeful. "Every girl in that school has loved Marcus Chance at one time or another," Cirri said matter-of-factly.

"Well, now you got him. What you gonna do with him?"

"I don't know."

"You not gonna have him for long."

Cirri grabbed the napkin and wiped the drool. Her eyes watched the TV, but her mind was on Marcus. She didn't feel an ounce of anger at him now. How could she have acted so mean to him this morning? She remembered how her hands had rounded over his firm, smooth shoulders, how his hands had run appreciatively down her body. She remembered him nudging her cheek this morning. He had wanted her. Why hadn't she let him come in just one more time? Maybe that would have been enough to make him come back to her this afternoon when school was out. Come back with his happy grin and his silly talk and bring the light back to her.

"There gonna be someone else next week for Marcus Chance, chile. Either that or six months at Lorton."

Cirri stopped bouncing Bryan. His face immediately puckered into a scream. "Come get your ol' baby," Cirri said.

Thea lunged up from the couch, her breasts swinging under the nightgown. "Don't be smart with me. I'm telling you the truth." She picked up the crying child and started for her bedroom. "Don't let him under your skin. He gonna hurt you, and you know it."

"Just cause he hurt you, don't mean I'm in for the same treatment," Cirri yelled.

"He didn't hurt me," Thea said, coming back. "What I had was a crush like every other girl in that school has had on that man. He never touched me. Never even saw me, I don't think. But you gone a lot further. You gonna let the crush crush you."

"No, ma'am."

"Uh huh. Your mama named you right, Cirrus James. Your head is in the clouds. Take it from me. Menfolks love us, but only for a little while."

What had Marcus said? Cirri sank back in the chair after Thea went into the bedroom. She tried to remember his words. Last night after the kids were asleep, and she and Marcus sat at the kitchen table flicking a piece of paper back and forth between them just for something to be doing, he said, "Well, what you think of Miz Brown, then?"

Cirri flicked the paper across to him. "She think she cool, but she too full of herself to really teach anybody anything. Mrs. Mitchell is the teacher I like. She knows what she doing. Besides Miz Brown plays favorites. She love you to death, for instance. That's why she always picking with you. That's her way of flirting."

He laughed and pushed the paper wad at her.

She shoved it back. "You think I'm lying?"

"No. You are Miss Honesty herself. And I like that."

She didn't exactly know what he had meant. But it sounded good, like he respected her in some way. And his eyes had been sincere. He had leaned up and taken her hands. The game with the paper was over. At that moment she had felt good, special. The memory of that moment was all she had as a brace against what Thea said, what Cirri herself knew to be true.

The baby was crying in the bedroom. Thea came out, marching to the kitchen in her nightgown. "Come on. I'm hungry. He's tired. He gonna have to cry hisself out. They's bologna or tuna fish."

"Bologna." Cirri got up from her thoughts gratefully. Without mentioning it, she and Thea helped each other in these little ways. Cirri gave Thea a hand with Bryan now and then. Thea gave Cirri lunch.

Thea opened the pantry closet and took out Cokes, potato chips, a pan of brownies. "Help yourself," she said.

"You ain't gonna lose the baby fat eating like that," Cirri said.

"You just a little minute of a thing standing there in your cute jeans, aren't you? That's all the lecture I need. Don't need no others, thank you."

Cirri smiled.

"I said when I got over them stitches I was gonna start my diet," Thea went on. "I figured I needed my nourishment to heal up good. Well, the spot still pulls."

Cirri spread mayonnaise on the bread. "Any excuse you like," she said.

The baby stopped crying all of a sudden and Thea, opening the bologna package, paused. Then she hurried to the bedroom. In a moment, the crying started again, and Thea came back out.

"Lord. He was going to sleep. But when he saw me he started up again."

Cirri cut the sandwiches and put them on plates.

Thea sank into a chair. "You hear about sudden baby deaths

and choking, Lord knows what all. Makes you a nervous wreck."

They ate while Bryan cried full force. Then he stopped again. Thea stared at Cirri, questioning and angry at the same time.

"He's all right," Cirri said. "Eat your lunch."

"I got to eat fast so I can get my bath and get dressed while he's still asleep. Maybe in a second I'll just tiptoe in and peek at him."

"When he's awake you're ready to kill him an' when he's asleep you're afraid he's dead," Cirri said.

"I know," Thea marveled. "That's the way it is."

Cirri finished her sandwich and watched Thea eat handfuls of potato chips. Cirri chewed a fingernail, debating whether or not she had the guts to ask Thea for money again. Thea always helped out, but Cirri had been asking too often lately and she knew it. "Thea, I need a few dollars."

"Chile, you know they's hardly nothing left in the bank as it is."

Once she'd made the decision to ask, Cirri was determined to get the money. "I know, but I put in for a job today at McDonald's. I'm gonna pay you back."

Thea narrowed her eyes. "What about school?"

"You know I don't go anyway. I'm here most days."

"So? You quitting?"

Cirri shrugged. "Just don't go."

"That's no decision."

"So?"

"A decision means you got to think about it."

"What's there to think about?"

"Think about being lonesome for one thing. If you wasn't coming 'round here, I'd go crazy. Ain't you lonesome on days you don't go to school and you don't come here?"

Cirri didn't want to think. "I need the money."

Thea lumbered into the living room and started pulling old paperback romances off a low shelf, leafing through them. Cirri knelt down and did the same. Thea's parents stuck money in the books when they had spare cash, more or less to hide it from themselves, as if it were in a bank. At the same time, it was also handy, if they needed it. She and Cirri had rifled through the books many times, sometimes lingering over the seductive covers of *Heart's Hidden Pleasures* or *The Lady in Green* or *A Man To Believe In*. Cirri intended to bring some money back, eventually, whenever she had any extra.

Thea found a dollar bill and laid it on the stained orange carpet, then replaced the book. Many books later, Cirri pulled out a five. It was a treasure. She raised her eyes to Thea.

"Take it." Thea sighed. "I got to get my bath."

"Thanks."

Thea nodded. Cirri let herself out.

At the Safeway she chose hamburg, a quart of milk, a small jar of peanut butter, margarine, and eggs. She added up the cost of each one before she put it in her basket, and saw that she had a few cents left over. She bought four penny gumballs out of the machine as a surprise for Pea and Willie.

When she climbed the stairs with the groceries, she stopped at Furry's, as usual. But this time she wasn't just looking for him or at the burned walls. The kitten was curled up in the corner, shivering. It raised its head when she stepped into the room but seemed too tired to come over to her.

She stepped across the garbage, stooped, and ran her fingertips down its little back. The kitten meowed as she picked it up, cuddled it next to her sweatshirt, and took it upstairs.

It explored the kitchen while she put the food away. She spoke to it in a cooing voice, then poured some milk into a bowl and sat down on the floor to watch. When it was finished, it licked its paws and wiped its face.

"You're a cutie, aren't you?" she whispered.

"A cat?" Mama asked, swaying in the doorway.

Cirri hadn't heard her get out of bed. "It's just a little one."

Mama walked in and slumped onto a kitchen chair. "Little ones grow into big ones," she said matter-of-factly. "We got any food, Cirri?"

After she slept like she was dead, she always wanted food. Usually the food made Mama feel better, took away the spinning she complained about, calmed the trembles in her hands. But she wouldn't eat if she had to fix it herself. The sight of uncooked food made her sicker. So Cirri cooked for her each day. If she went to school, Mama didn't eat at all. Cirri was glad to have something to give Mama today. "I could scramble you some eggs."

"Oh that would taste good, baby," Mama said, holding her head up with one hand as if she felt sick.

Cirri busied herself with the eggs, toasted some bread on the stove burner, slathered it with margarine and jelly. She poured Mama a little milk, although she probably wouldn't drink it. Cirri could put it back in the fridge later for the kids.

When Cirri put the food down, steaming, in front of Mama, she grabbed Cirri's hand. "Thank you, baby. I got to get me off this stuff." Her head bobbed. "This stuff make me feel so bad." She ran her fingers up into her hair, held her head again. "Makes me want to die."

"Eat something," Cirri said gently. She patted Mama's arm. She lifted a forkful of eggs and Mama took a bite.

Now came the crying. Tears started down Mama's face. "You taking such good care of me, honey."

Twice before, when Mama was like this, Cirri had mentioned the drug treatment clinic near her school. But Mama had pulled back. "No! They get you in there, take your name, take your kids away from you, turn you in to the po-lice. I ain't leavin' my babies behind." So Cirri didn't talk about the clinic anymore. She just listened and tried to take care of Mama.

Mama was still crying. Cirri wished she could let out her own tears, too. Every day Mama almost fooled her into crying, except that Cirri had come to know that it wasn't really Mama talking and feeling lost. It was the stuff talking, making her head spin, making her hate it for a little while. Soon it would make her start wanting it again. Probably she wanted it right now. Underneath everything else, probably it was whispering to her, "Don't cry, Ruby. Come to me."

Cirri held up more eggs. Mama wiped her face with her sleeve and took a bite. She picked up the toast and ate some of that on her own. Cirri got up and shook out some of the still damp laundry, and turned it over on the chair backs.

"You been washing," Mama said, a quaver in her voice.

"Yeah, but it's not dry yet."

"Um huh."

"You should wear them brown pants soon as they get dry. It's cold out these nights."

They talked about Mama going out like this every day, as if she were going to a night job or something. A couple of times Cirri had tried to get her to stay home, had held her at the door. Mama had said, "What is your problem, girl?" Her whole body had quivered and felt tight with need. "I'm just going down the street. They's a little party at Peejay's."

Cirri had clapped her hands over her ears and watched Mama's lips keep moving. She didn't want to know where Mama went or what she did to get her stuff or what lies she was telling. And every day Cirri hoped Mama would at least eat something and dress warmly enough and make it home in the morning.

While Mama finished the eggs, Cirri picked up the kitten and stroked it until it fell asleep. Its relaxed warmth on her legs was comforting.

"I'm gone clean myself up," Mama said, standing, steadying herself with the table.

This was the time, for a little while, that Mama thought she was all right. She would get herself washed up, comb her dirty hair, maybe put on some lipstick. Then she would sit in front of the TV and act like her hands weren't shaking. Her eyes would follow the show, but her head would wobble. Soon she would get up and wander off, looking for the filthy coat, act like she was just going to get a pack of cigarettes. Then she would leave.

Cirri ran her fingers down the back of the scrawny kitten who was curled up asleep in her lap. She stared at the dirty dishes on the table, the untouched milk. Grape jelly was stuck on the plate like an infected sore. She would have to clean it up. Cook the food, clean it up, beg for the money to buy it. And Mama was getting worse. Cirri hated it. All of it. She couldn't do one damned thing more.

With one swipe, she knocked the dishes to the floor. The plate skittered and broke. Milk splattered the walls and floor. Dutifully, the little kitten jumped down and began licking up the mess.

Cirri met Pea and Willie at the bus stop. She handed them the gumballs and told them there was another surprise for them back at the house.

"Mama there?" Pea asked, excited.

"No. She gone already," Cirri answered. "It's another surprise."

"Marcus," Willie guessed.

"You won't be able to guess what it is, so stop trying."

"I know," Pea shouted. "It's Furry."

"Law, chile, what did I just say to you?"

"You're playing with us," Pea said and tilted her head to look slyly at Cirri.

Cirri shook her head.

"It's Furry!" Willie screamed and started to run toward their building with Pea following close behind him.

Cirri caught up with them at the open door of Furry's apartment. They stared in at the dark, smelly cold.

"He's in our house, then," Willie yelled and bounded up the stairs.

"You kids is crazy," Cirri shouted after them.

They knocked on the door and waited impatiently while Cirri ambled up with the key. "Ain't no Furry in here," she crooned.

The kids burst through the door then stood still, disappointed.

"I tole you," Cirri said and flipped on the TV.

"Well, what's our surprise then?" Willie wailed.

"You said there was a surprise, Cirri."

"Oh, you wanna see your surprise?" she asked. "Well, I don't know exactly where it is myself."

"What?" The kids looked around the room for anything new.

"But when I left it was on Mama's bed."

They rushed in and she went with them because she wanted to see their faces. The kitten was still asleep on the bed.

"Oh, a kitty!" Pea screamed and hopped on the bed beside it.

"Be quiet!" Willie scolded in a whisper. "You're gonna wake

it up." The kitten blinked its eyes. "See. I tole you. You woke it up!"

"It wanted to see us," Pea said.

"But it's just a baby. Babies need their sleep. Isn't that right, Cirri?"

"Yeah, but it's been sleeping a lot. I think it's all right to wake it up."

Willie promptly picked up the kitten and touched its tiny pink nose to his.

"Can we keep it?" Pea asked.

"It's yours and Willie's," Cirri said with a smile.

Pea jumped off the bed and threw her arms around Cirri's waist.

She fried three hamburgers for supper and put them each between two slices of white bread. She poured the last of the milk into glasses and regretted wasting the milk that she had knocked to the floor this afternoon. Now there would be none for breakfast or for the kitten. They discussed names for the kitten and had just settled on Furry when Marcus knocked on the door.

She hadn't expected him to come or she would have fixed up. She would have been thinking about him, getting herself ready with words, sweet things to say to let him know how glad she was to see him, how much she regretted being mad this morning. But he walked in unexpectedly and took her off guard.

Her throat ached like she wanted to cry, just seeing him again. But what came out of her mouth was, "Well, you could of let somebody know you was coming."

"Should I of called?"

She lifted a shoulder. "Sent a telegram."

"We got a kitten, Marcus," Pea announced.

"We don't know if it's a boy or a girl," Willie added, "so we named it Furry."

"Furry's a boy's name," Pea objected.

"It ain't either," Willie argued. "It's just that our friend is named Furry, but that ain't like Jack. Jack's a real boy's name."

"What you doing back over here anyhow?" Cirri demanded of Marcus. She couldn't understand herself. Everything came out sounding mad.

But he didn't seem to notice. "Brought you some groceries. I ain't eating fried chicken for breakfast again."

He held up two big bags, but instead of thanking him, she said, "Oh yeah? What you doing? Moving in?"

He pulled her out of the kitchen, away from the kids, and kissed her hard on the lips. "You ain't the only woman I kissed today," he whispered. "You jealous?"

She pushed him away. "Jealous over something like you? I ain't *even* got the time."

He laughed, grabbed her again and held her. "I also kissed my grandmom this afternoon when I got home from school. She's a beautiful lady."

Cirri didn't know whether or not to be relieved. His joke cut too close.

"Can I stay tonight?" he murmured.

"We got a bed."

He grinned at her. "Don't cut me one inch a slack, Cirri James. Okay, now? No slack."

She turned back into the kitchen. "I'm listenin', dahlin'."

Heck

THERE WERE TIMES LIKE this—when Heck Jasper shambled into school early, past the leaves and litter around the steps, past the graffiti on the sidewalks, through the clanging metal doors—that he felt he was entering a citadel. The janitors had done their work; the floors were clean, the walls in the lobby were streaked only with the natural gray curves and veins of the marble, not the bloodred and neon of the slogans sprayed outside. The building smelled of routine and order, if not exactly of high productivity. For the ninety years of its existence, the school had held strong.

Heck climbed the stairs. Any wise defender knew to locate the strongest fortification, the command post, high and centered. His office was on the second of the three floors, in the middle of the square of classrooms, offices, labs, workshops and storage rooms.

He turned on lights with his key as he went because it was

November-morning dark. Fluorescents flickered on in the trophy case, and spots lit up the dusty flags. But there were corners and recesses down the long corridor that the old lights didn't illuminate. These would be flooded with sunlight later, sunlight through the grills over the huge wooden casement windows, sunlight that made the walls gleam.

It was because of citadels, strongholds and trenches that he'd gotten into this business in the first place. Fortifications and defenses had fascinated him as a kid. He had started with the First World War, the one his father had told him stories about, and he worked his way back—through the Civil War, the Revolutions, the Crusades, to Troy and the Biblical battles. He had learned all he could about weaponry, strategy, causes, decorations for valor. It was as familiar to him as family. So he had chosen history in college. What else is history about but the conflicts and the conflagrations? And what other practical thing could a man do with history but teach it? He had taught history for ten years and gradually moved up in the system to be a principal.

He unlocked the door to the office and turned on the lights. Four desks occupied this outer area—one for each of the two secretaries, one for the attendance officer, one for his assistant principal. Lined against one wall were the straight-backed wooden chairs where students slumped as they waited to be questioned, harangued, suspended by him. He was the general of discipline. The opposite wall was lined with file cabinets full of methodically kept records. District maps hung on the wall above. Attendance graphs showed averages of twenty-five to thirty-five percent of the school's students missing daily.

He gazed at these a moment, his briefcase weighty at the end of his arm. Sixty-three years old—his hair was white for Chrissake—and he had been battling kids, trying to knock something into their heads, for a long time. When he had first started teaching, there weren't any black principals or assistant principals except in black systems. Everyone had said, "Let the kids see black leadership and they'll study." It had been almost a promise. Brown v. the Board of Education, years of struggle after that, and now here he was, a black man leading a predominantly black school. And still the kids didn't study, not much anyway, black or white.

There wasn't much of anything academic that captured their attention, made them curious, made them think. All those old generals—Hannibal, Napoleon, Sherman, MacArthur—were amazing. Their times were full of intrigue, glory, cruelty. But most kids didn't want to hear about it. They didn't want to hear about government, even though they lived in Washington, D.C. They didn't want to hear about math facts or percentages either, about life science or novels or nutrition or even sex.

What they had on their minds amazed and sometimes scared him. They were angry and bored and desperate. But they didn't know they were desperate. Heck alternated between being pissed off at them and feeling sorry for them. It was the times. These times made kids desperate.

He was tired this morning, as usual. He couldn't sleep many nights, worrying or just thinking. When he was tired, he started dwelling on those boyhood ghosts of generals and wars, battles more easily fought and won. He knew he was a little daft to be harking back to all that. But it came unbidden, a sign of age, he thought.

His father had run a barber shop. He had returned from France in 1919, worked odd jobs for a while till he could save up a little money, then rented the corner shop where he had worked for the rest of his life. His buddies from the District's First Separate Battalion were steady customers. They trusted one another, went out of their way for one another, and every now and then, chewed over old times together. Young Heck, sweeping up or shining the mirrors, would slow down and listen as the former soldiers rehearsed the battles.

"If he'd a ran us across the hill, we'd a had the cover of the hedge," one would say.

"Cover or no cover, the flank was exposed. No way 'round that."

"And going straight up was the fastest way."

"Fastest way to meet your Maker."

"Maker don't care about no flanks."

They had fought with a French battalion. Of the 480 Washingtonians, 25 had come back with the Croix de Guerre. It was a simpler fight in many ways than what Heck had on his hands. They had faced a clear-cut enemy, strove for a well-defined goal. You either won or lost. And there were awards. In Heck's business of education, there were no decorations for bravery.

He unlocked the door to his office and was surprised to find the light already on. His hand had automatically moved to the switch but stopped in midair. The room had been ransacked.

At one time the office must have been a stately chamber of dark wood paneling, heavy drapes, expensive furniture and glass-doored bookshelves. But the wood had long since been painted over with heavy coats of institutional yellow, and the windows were bare of drapery. Heck had the standard-issue gray metal desk and swivel chair. All that had remained of the original ninety-year-old office were the bookshelves and their glass doors. Heck had been extremely proud of them.

Now the glass sparkled in thousands of shards on the linoleum. Every pane had been shattered. Broken glass littered the books, the shelves, the tops of filing cabinets. The drawers to the cabinets that held the confidential, permanent records of students and staff were open, the contents strewn about. He tiptoed through the glass to his desk. It was bare except for an empty Coke can and a paper basket that had held french fries. Ketchup was smeared in the bottom of it. Something sticky had been spilled on top of the desk. Swept onto the floor were his telephone, family pictures, files, papers, IN and OUT baskets, letters, everything. Behind the desk, the computer was upside down on the floor, the screen smashed.

He stepped carefully to the back door of his office, which he rarely opened. It was open now, leading to a small inner corridor that gave into the guidance counselors' offices. Heck unlocked the first office. Nothing was out of place. He opened two others which were also untouched. The damage seemed limited to his office. He plodded back, trying to think of who and why. One or two people came to mind, but he couldn't imagine that they would have the gall to do this.

On closer examination, he saw that the back door had not been damaged, and the lock was intact. The front door was also undamaged. The intruders must have had a set of keys. If so, what else had they smashed up or stolen? His first thought was of the new computer room.

Fifteen computers, new last year. With the software and printers, they had cost over a hundred thousand dollars. The thought of them destroyed made him light-headed.

But when he switched on the light, every computer was in place, the chairs pushed in, the floor spotless. He stood and gawked in gratitude.

What other room might they have gotten into? What else was valuable? The A-V room was in the basement next to the elevator. He took the stairs; they were faster.

Projectors, videotape players, TVs, tape recorders. Wouldn't the neighbors have seen them carrying things out? Heck knew all the neighbors around the school. They tolerated the kids scooping snow off their small lawns for snowball

battles in the winter. They put up with the loudspeaker announcements on the football field in the fall, with the litter
and the rowdiness and the traffic. He always thanked them for
accepting the thousand teenagers who converged on their
street each day. In return, they called him sometimes with little problems and complaints—the knot of students that always
hung out in the nearby alley, the suspicious goings-on near
the north wall of the school. Wouldn't they have called if they
saw TVs and other equipment being toted out late at night?

His hands shook as he tried to slide the key in the A-V
room lock. But as with the computer room all the equipment
sat there untouched and gleaming.

Heck leaned against the wall in the darkened corridor and
worried whether the attack had been directed only at him.
Why hadn't the vandals stolen anything? Or maybe they had.
Permanent records and files were in his office. But if someone
wanted to take one of those, they would have done it secretly.
Why draw attention with all that destruction?

He had one more thought. There was a considerable
amount of cash in the cafeteria—money from lunches, money
to make change. It was sent downtown at the end of each
week. Today, midweek, there would be a few hundred dollars
in the metal box. But he didn't rush to check as he had rushed
to the other rooms. He trudged down the hall, thinking that
even if the money was gone, why had they found it necessary
to destroy his office, to break everything in it? They had to
have been making a statement. A statement to him, about him.

Plenty of kids had threatened him over the years. "I'm
gonna get you, man." "You ain't nothing, Jasper." "You
messin' up my life. You gonna be sorry." Someone had once
broken the windshield of his car with a baseball bat. There'd
been an incident with spray paint. But no one had ever
stormed the headquarters of the citadel.

In fact, often in the past, he had been able to win over the kids who had threatened him. Not all of them, of course. You couldn't win all the battles, and you had to choose your fights carefully. But lots of times, once they had gotten over their anger, once they had accepted his discipline, he had lavished them with extra attention, and they usually had come around.

Some of them came back—now, after twenty-five years—and thanked him. "You okay, Dr. Jasper." "You were a hard man, but you were right." "You were better than a father to me."

He had always hoped he had been doing a good job—the best he could in this neighborhood of poor families and too much crime, of kids half-loved and half-cared-for. Then three years ago, when he had been so sick with the heart operation and thought he should retire, he had received over a hundred letters at the hospital, pleading with him to stay on. Parents, former and current students, neighbors and community friends urged him to get well and get back to Grant. The one that he had put to memory said, "You have been a pillar of strength and stability in our community, a wise and conscientious leader. Please stay on at the high school. How could we ever replace you?"

He had been won over by their numbers and their kindness. If he had ever had any doubts about what he might have accomplished at Grant or what he meant to people, those letters had helped to allay them.

The school had staged a surprise assembly on the day he returned to work. The superintendent, who had also received letters supporting him, came. The school band played. The choir sang. The auditorium overflowed with friends, faculty and parents. The students were entirely well behaved. The superintendent announced that he hoped Heck would agree not to get sick for another fifty years because everyone was convinced that Grant's walls would tumble down without Heck there to hold them up.

It had been more acclaim and flattery than any principal usually received or deserved. He had been moved, and he had told them so. Then he had barked that it was time to get back to work

Now, he slowly unlocked the doors to the cafeteria office, turned on the lights, and opened the cabinet where Mrs. Hempley hid the money box behind the huge cans of peaches. Nothing was amiss. Mrs. Hempley had the only key to the money box, but he could tell by its weight that the money was inside.

He was in no hurry this time as he walked toward the elevator. He would give his legs a rest. But as the elevator carried him to the second floor, he felt his heart start to race. And when he reentered his destroyed office, the blood was screaming in his ears.

The vandalism had been an act of hate, a raging curse meant especially for him. Heck knew that what he had feared was coming true. He wasn't as effective as he used to be. He was losing his strength. He was losing his power in the school. He was assailable.

Outside the school walls, things had changed in the last quarter century, even more so in the last few years. The Washington of national government was fine, always was, always would be. But the Washington of neighborhoods was dying. The people who happened to live within a walk of the Capitol and the White House were suffering. He saw it every day.

The children were victims, but they had no sense of that. They just knew they had to be tough. They had to be savvy in the ways of the streets. They knew they had to grab what they could in life because life could be very short. Too many of them had seen older friends or brothers sent away to prison or killed. So they were selfish and intolerant of one another and cynical. And they brought all that to school.

He had been running the school the same way for twenty-five years, as a big, extended family, like the one he had come from. He was the head of that family. He demanded order and respect. He dispensed discipline, care and concern. For a long time his approach had worked. Only recently had he begun to feel he was losing ground. He was getting weaker just as the outside forces were getting stronger. It seemed like the barbarians would soon overrun the place. He looked around his office. Maybe they already had.

He retreated to the outer office, sat down with a groan and called the police. Then he tried to anticipate their questions. Who would have done this, and why? The french fries suggested a student. A half dozen were capable of such a rageful act—kids he had suspended recently, expelled, even a couple he had testified against in court. Tension in the building sometimes was as thick and palpable as heavy smoke rising from the fires outside, fires that society had allowed to smolder and looked to the schools to cool.

As the first and final melting pot, the publicly funded agency of upliftment, the American opportunity machine, the educational system was supposed to produce good citizens who were prepared to work, pay taxes, and not be problems. But they were already problems when they arrived at the school. Try as he might, he often couldn't change that in three years' time.

He stared at the undamaged office door. What about one of the teachers, some of whom had keys which they lent to one another? A teacher could have gotten hold of the office key, planted the Coke and fries, and had a ball with the glass doors. But who? And why?

He rubbed his temples and rotated his head to loosen the tight muscles in his neck. He had to focus more. He had to defend against the intruding, distracting memories and concentrate on the present.

Dr. Canaletti, associate superintendent for Grant's district, had called to tell Heck to meet him at noon. Now Heck waited impatiently in the outer office and watched Canaletti's secretary type on the computer.

Canaletti had a varied background. He had started out as a priest, teaching sociology and economics at a premier Jesuit high school in New York. Then he had renounced his vows for whatever reason caused a man to turn his back on something he had sworn to God to devote his life to, and he became a businessman. Specifically, he became the head of a small company that sold educational products—pull-down maps, math puzzles, creative-writing kits. He must have done well there because within three years he had leapfrogged to a much bigger company—a biomedical company. And it was there he apparently had made his mark as a shrewd, adaptable, successful administrator. Why he had come back to education Heck didn't know. But the superintendent had introduced Leo Canaletti last year as "the man who will bring acumen and accountability to that district." Now Heck was about to be held accountable.

Heck had met with Canaletti before at principals' meetings. At the first one, Canaletti had handed out his résumé. "I haven't come here via the regular route, as you can see," he had said. "I don't know if this background qualifies me to be an associate superintendent, but here I am, and I'm going to give it my best shot. I think what I *do* bring is a fresh perspective and a few tricks about getting behemoths to move. I'm not talking about you, but about the bureaucracy."

He had gone on to talk about test scores, his new dividends. He talked about incentives, bonuses, performance peaks—a system of rewards for students, teachers and schools for improving test scores.

Heck was interested in him as a man who had been successful in two careers so far and was embarking on a third. The résumé did not indicate whether Canaletti was married or not. But he had obviously adjusted to life among the worldly in all other respects. He was twenty years younger than Heck, full of confidence and ideas.

When the previous associate super had resigned, Heck had entertained thoughts of being tapped for Canaletti's job. Heck was the most senior of the principals in his district. He knew the district, the school system, the parents, the kids. But the superintendent hadn't even looked inside the system. He wanted that fresh perspective, he had said.

Heck told himself that he didn't want the job anyway. It was all paperwork and headaches. He liked the exposure to the kids. He liked being entirely in charge of his own microcosm at Grant. Who needed a tremendous and burdensome new challenge? At his age, with all but one of his five children gone, and the daily routines at school and home so well established and easy, why should he want to rock the boat? What he wanted was to relax.

He crossed his knees and looked at his watch. Twelve-ten. It wasn't right that he be kept waiting. He felt himself getting angry, felt his chest and throat tighten.

But the man was white. That rankled. What did he know about the city, the district, the problems of these kids and their families? His was a fresh perspective, all right—so fresh as to be half-baked.

At twelve-fifteen Canaletti exploded from his office and was standing before Heck in two strides, hand thrust out.

"I'm very sorry, Dr. Jasper. Come in, please."

He was in his shirtsleeves and his tie was loose, his collar unbuttoned. He indicated a chair, then lit a cigarette with the swiftness and agility of a man who had done it many times before. He sat at his desk, intent, and said, "Give me the details."

Heck couldn't leave behind the tension and anger of the wait. He spoke sharply. "I came in this morning. My office was a shambles. Every pane of glass in my bookshelves broken."

"What were they after?"

"I have no idea."

"Other damage in the school?"

"None."

"How'd they get in?"

"The police think they had a key."

"How many people have keys to your office? Or to the school for that matter?"

"Too many, I guess."

Canaletti smiled, inhaled deeply, then sprang up and started pacing, as he did at meetings, behind Heck's chair.

"Are any files missing?"

"We don't know yet."

"What else is missing?"

"Nothing. I can't imagine what they might have wanted."

"Think!"

Heck turned and stopped Canaletti with his raised voice. "I have thought! Wouldn't you, if someone came in here and smashed up everything?" Heck gestured around the room, but realized there was nothing as nice in the associate superintendent's office as there had been in his own. There were gray metal bookshelves and file cabinets, a gray metal desk, dusty venetian blinds, endless stacks of papers on every surface.

That awareness made Heck think he might be missing something in thinking about the crime because he had so loved his office. "Maybe someone was trying to get back at me."

"Threats?"

Heck shrugged.

"Even those you dismissed as casual," Canaletti prompted.

Heck shook his head. "Kids say things all the time when they're mad."

Canaletti's chair squeaked when he sat down again. "From my point of view, you are dealing with several problems at Grant. Correct me if I'm wrong. Attendance, deadwood in the faculty, drugs on the outside. All contributing to academic problems, and thus to low test scores. Would you agree?"

"Those are some of the problems," Heck began. "There is also family disruption, kids bearing the responsibility of adults, a city out of control with murders . . ."

"Our job doesn't include the whole city," Canaletti interrupted.

"But what happens in the city affects us."

"Yes, but you have to define and deal with only what goes on behind the closed doors of your school."

"I do." Heck defended himself. "But I don't think success can or should be measured only in terms of test scores. Those kids have lots of things going on in their lives."

"Test scores are an objective measure, after all. And we're mandated to turn kids out knowing certain basic facts and processes. If they don't know them, we've failed. Yes, we hope that we'll also have taught them to love learning and to deal responsibly with life. But those goals aren't measurable. We must stick to the task at hand."

"Maybe you're mandated to get test results. But I feel mandated to try to do something more meaningful for them. Not just cram them with useless information for a test."

Canaletti rose and started pacing again. "Partly I'm playing the devil's advocate," he said. "I know you aren't excited with my push for scores. That's a difference between us. I have to show results. But, I'm trying to show you that it's possible to take a tougher stance."

"I need to be tougher?"

"Come on. We all know that sometimes learning is boring, sometimes it's hard work and doesn't have any immediate relevance. But we have got to teach these students that meeting the challenge will stand them in good stead in the long run."

That line of reasoning worked, Heck thought, wherever it was that Canaletti came from. But here, everything was stacked against the kids. And the pitiful part was that Canaletti didn't realize it. Things had been stacked against black kids for a long time now.

When Heck was in high school, 1943, he had worked for the War Department, waiting for the day when he could join up to fight. He worked long hours beside boys his own age, white boys who seemed to know so much more than he did about math and history and geography. Yet Heck was one of the best students in his school. All the schools were segregated in those days, but he hadn't thought that much about it until he began talking to his teachers.

"Don't you understand?" they said. "Open your eyes and look around you. Our schools can't measure up to theirs. We've got fifty children in some of our classes. Those children come from all over this country from poor and backward places 'cause rumor has it things just gotta be better in the capital city. Some of those kids, sixteen, eighteen years old, can't read or write because schools where they came from were so poor. We teachers can't take care of all those backward children, so we set you good students to helping them. The time you spend doing that is time you're not learning things on your own level. Do you think it's like that in their schools?

"No, they have got books. Up-to-date books. And twenty, twenty-five children per class. All of them know their three R's by the time they get to high school. So the teachers can teach the advanced stuff."

Canaletti caring only about test scores was another cheat, Heck thought, just like when he was in high school. The tests were on SAT-type vocabulary, on grammar, on algebra and world geography—things that suburban kids, kids in wealthier districts had been learning for a while now. It would be nice if the kids from Grant knew that stuff. But it would be even better if they were solid with their simple reading, writing and reasoning so they could be literate adults. It would be better if they came to school every day of the week and didn't have to work night jobs to help support their families. It would be better if they didn't have to be afraid to walk through their neighborhoods and if they could have nutritious food to eat three meals a day. It would be better if their parents were well educated and helped them out with their studies and made them do their homework. But that was generally the least of their parents' worries. The test scores weren't going to rise until Canaletti and all those above him realized these things, realized that not much had actually changed in forty or fifty years' time, except maybe had gotten worse.

Heck sighed. "I can tell the teachers to push harder for test results. But that's not what's needed."

"A lot of people in this country from the Secretary of Education on down, would disagree," said Canaletti. "They want to see city scores go up. I don't know why we can't make that happen, unless teachers and administrators aren't doing their jobs."

"I'm doing my job," Heck said loudly. "I resent you insin-uating otherwise. I run that school as I see fit. The kids need material that they can use, that fits in with their lives, that helps them in the here and now, that's interesting so that maybe they'll come to school tomorrow and the next day. I encourage my teachers to drill and prepare students for the tests once in a while, but I will not let them do a steady diet of it. And if our scores don't rise, so be it."

Canaletti leaned back, took a deep breath. "Yes, Dr. Jasper, I'd say we have a definite difference of opinions."

Heck had spoken his mind, but he felt that somehow, in the end, Canaletti would get his way.

Canaletti lit another cigarette and threw the lighter onto the desk. "Different subject. Teachers. I hear there's a lot of deadwood in this district. Evaluations are due to me this week. Could a teacher have gotten into your office? Maybe did all the damage out of rage and made some changes on their sheets?"

Heck laughed. "Those sheets don't mean anything. The way the categories are set up, I can give them the lowest rat-ings and, if they just show up ninety-five percent of the time, they get a satisfactory. Anyway, why a teacher?"

"Keys."

"I can't picture it."

Canaletti squinted against the smoke. "Someone breaks into and destroys the principal's office. Makes it look like it's not a tight ship. That's all I'm saying. See what I mean?"

Test scores and appearances. Canaletti was a superficial man. Heck nodded. "I see."

"I'm not releasing this to the media," Canaletti said, getting up to signal the end of the meeting. "Neither of us needs this."

* * *

Heck's knees hurt, as they usually did, at the end of the day. Mornings were better. But by evening, after climbing up and down the stairs at school, walking miles of hallway, his knees felt ready to buckle.

He unlocked the front door to his house, hung up his coat and jacket, took off his tie, all the while playing out the string of his thoughts, back to his meeting with Canaletti, back to the discovery of his office this morning, back to his own school days nearly half a century ago.

He turned on a lamp in the living room and eased himself onto the couch, put his feet up on a footstool. The rickets had bowed his legs when he was a kid, and each year they hurt a little more. Back in the days of the Depression, blacks were last hired, first fired. Heck's father was lucky to be self-employed, but too many of his customers couldn't pay to have their hair cut by a barber anymore. They came to talk, as always, and his father was glad of that, but there was no jingle in their pockets.

So his mother had decided to take in boarders to raise a little money. With all the Southerners migrating to the federal city, where they supposed there would be greater opportunities, housing was scarce. She rented out the big back bedroom to the Harrises, from Georgia. The rent included the evening meal that the families took together in the Jaspers' dining room.

Mr. Harris could keep up on the rent only about half the time, there was so little work to be found. But they were doing the best they could, and Heck's mother declined to put them on the street. As time went on, the evening meal became more and more meager. His mother didn't apologize when she set the tureen of greens and onions cooked with a little bacon in the middle of the table and dished up equal portions into each person's china bowl. And no one complained, either.

She controlled dinnertimes, but on the front porch after-
wards, Heck's father ruled. While the women washed the
dishes, Mr. Harris, Heck's father, and any number of other
gentlemen from the neighborhood gathered on the porch to
talk. Sometimes one of them would have a little extra money
to buy smokes, which he shared. Heck and the other boys
would sit on the steps and listen or play games in the spindly
grass of the postage-stamp yard while the men traded stories
and jokes.

"You hear what they saying at the employment office?"

"Naw, what?"

"Don't have to worry about colored men not having work."

"Why's that?"

"We used to starving. Like sailors. They used to drowning."

They told each other about work opportunities they had
heard of. They wondered about the stability of the government and of the president, whose car they saw flashing
through town.

Off and on there was talk about "advancement." For long
months, dedicated people picketed two branches of the local
People's Drug Store that served an entirely black clientele but
had no black employees. The pickets went on to no avail.
Then in 1937, the CIO broke away from the AFL in order to
admit all workers, no matter what shade of skin. The men on
the porch said, "Good. Let People's old Drug do what they
want. We makin' some advancement in the CIO."

But by and large, none of the men on the porch did anything for advancement except talk about it. Heck's father
would smoke and stare out at the street when the subject came
up. He'd comment sometimes, but mostly he'd sit quietly. And
Heck knew why his father didn't like the subject. "I don't need
them people," he said, talking about whites. "An' they don't
need me. So be it."

He had been shot through the shoulder in France, charging that hill under orders. But he had kept fighting and captured a unit of fifteen enemy soldiers single-handedly later in the day. "By nightfall," he said, "I wasn't exactly in my right mind." The doctors had had to remove a good part of the shattered bones and ligaments and he had spent weeks battling the infections. He had been awarded the Croix de Guerre and looked forward to the homecoming at the end of the war. But D.C.'s big parade for the returning soldiers, led by President Wilson, was held before the black District's First Separate Battalion even got back.

Two years later, the Lincoln Memorial was dedicated, and Heck's father attended. The festivities of the day for the Great Emancipator were segregated. Even the keynote speaker, Dr. Robert Moen, president of Tuskegee Institute, was not allowed to sit on the dais. He had had to wait with all the other colored folk in the swampy area to the far left of the memorial.

Three years after that, Washington hosted the Ku Klux Klan. They paraded, 25,000-strong, in their sheets, down Pennsylvania Avenue and held a formal ceremony at the Washington Monument.

In 1938, when Heck was eleven, his mother's brother and family had arrived unannounced from North Carolina. Heck's uncle had no work, and things were very bad down there. Houses were being burned and black men were being lynched. He had two baby girls; his wife was pregnant. Heck's mother took them in.

Mr. Harris had drawn Heck's father aside on the porch one evening. "You been helping us out considerable when I can't make the rent. But now, with your kin here, I 'spect you'll be needing that room. We'll be moving out."

"Where to?" Heck's father had asked.

"We'll find us a place."

His father considered a few minutes. "No. I'd rather you didn't."

"Why not?"

Heck's father managed to find a way to make it seem that he wasn't helping out. "I'm just afraid that my barbering by itself won't bring in enough to keep us going. With two men in the house, and now three, I think we can make a go of it."

Three men, three families, seventeen mouths to feed. There hadn't been that much to eat. Heck stared at his legs up on the footstool. The bones curved.

He rested his head on the back of the couch, wishing Yvonne were home. But she wouldn't be home for an hour, by the time she left her office at the hospital and then fought the rush-hour traffic over to this side of the city.

They had moved into Grant's district when Heck had been appointed principal twenty-five years ago. The house was cheap for its size because the location was undesirable. But Heck believed in living in the school's neighborhood, and they needed a large house. There were three babies then. Kate and Tina weren't born yet. The house had been old and broken down, and for years they had worked on it—stripping filthy wallpaper, patching plaster, painting, installing weather-tight windows, sanding floors, eventually remodeling the kitchen. He had enjoyed the weekend work. Yvonne had good taste. The rooms had become livable and lovely.

One by one, the children had graduated from Grant and left home. Hector Junior, their oldest, had gone to Howard Medical School. He was a doctor now in New York. John was in graduate school, studying foreign policy at American University. Edward was in the Peace Corps in Ceylon. Katie was a senior at Wellesley, an English major. Only Tina was home, a junior at Grant.

The neighborhood had been changing in the last few years. Their street, with several other of these big old houses, had started to attract investors. Values had gone up. He ran his hand across the white damask couch that Yvonne had recently had reupholstered. They had done well. They had launched five children into the world. They had a comfortable, attractive home. They had each other and good jobs. Why had he ever coveted Canaletti's job or Canaletti's life?

He closed his eyes. Tina should be home soon from wherever she was—some after-school activity. He expected to hear her at the door any minute, but for just this second he was glad to rest his eyes and his knees. He worried about Tina. She was in a rebellious stage. But then, he had worried about all of his children at one time or another. He drifted off to sleep.

When he heard the door, he called out, "Tina?"

"No, it's me," Yvonne answered. She hung up her coat, then came and kissed him.

"Tina home?"

"I don't know. I just got here."

He glanced at his watch, more asleep than awake. "You wouldn't believe the day I've had," he said and went on to tell Yvonne all that had happened. "Canaletti wants me to toughen up," he concluded. "Thinks I'm soft."

"He doesn't know you, then."

He sat up straighter, trying to shake the fatigue that wouldn't let him go. "This incident says that I'm what's wrong at Grant because the attack was directed at me." He remembered his feelings from the morning. He was losing control; he was getting weaker just at a time that demanded more strength.

"Is he trying to kick you out?"

"If he threw me out or had me transferred, it would be as much as admitting that there were big problems at Grant, which he doesn't want to do. Not yet, anyway. He might use that later to get himself off the hook if he doesn't get the results he's been promising." Heck wasn't fighting. He was just holding on. And he knew it.

"You've had bozo associates before and handled them."

That was true. Heck nodded and remembered how angry Canaletti had made him that morning: the wait in the outer office, telling Heck to think about who had vandalized his office when he obviously *had* thought about it, Canaletti's absurd demand for test scores when the kids barely even made it to school half the time. "He's a new kind of bozo. He talks about kids as if they're products. This year's product has suddenly got to be new and improved. It's a version of 'Speed up the wagon through the cotton field; make the slaves pick faster.' The boss will have his results; what'll the pickers have? A lot of useless facts for a test. I hate white men, especially dumb white men."

Yvonne stroked his cheek. "You're letting him get to you."

He heard the door, saw Tina put her books down on the stairs. He stood up. He didn't want to be coddled. He wanted to feel what Canaletti felt when he paced. He strode to the fireplace. "That's right! He's getting to me because he might know business, but he doesn't know *my* business."

When Tina started up the stairs, Heck said, "Where are you going, young lady?"

"Upstairs," she said sullenly.

"Where have you been?" he demanded. How could he control things at school when he seemed to have lost control even at home? "It's nearly six-thirty. You know you're supposed to be home before that."

"I was at the library. Studying." She batted her eyelashes

once, slowly, as if he was nothing. "Want the phone numbers of witnesses?"

Yvonne intervened. "Daddy's had a hard day."

"I know. I saw his office."

"So, why don't you come down here and talk to us?" Yvonne asked.

"I just wanted to relax a little, Mom."

"Why don't you help with dinner?" Heck suggested. "Then we can *all* relax at the table."

"*You* won't relax," she said.

"Come down here!"

She rolled her eyes and sashayed down to him.

Heck spoke in a hoarse whisper of frustration. "It was fine if you've been off studying, but your grades tell me otherwise. Don't lie to me, Quintina. Where have you been?"

"At the library."

"Mrs. Barnes can confirm that?"

"I don't know if Mrs. Barnes saw me or not. She was busy at the desk."

"Did you check out any books?"

"No."

"You were out last night, too."

"At Patricia Goodson's. Go ahead. Call her. We were working on a speech for English."

Yvonne intervened and spoke to Tina. "Go wash your hands and fix a salad for supper." After Tina walked away, Yvonne said. "That was serving no purpose except to antagonize her."

"She's got an attitude that she hasn't had before, and I don't like it."

"Okay, but talk to her sometime when you're not trying to prove something to yourself or to Canaletti."

"That has nothing to do with it."

"You're frustrated and mad. And Tina's been getting on my nerves too. But tonight's not the night to get it all straightened out."

"I might as well start by getting tough in my own home."

"That's what I mean. Stop thinking about him. Forget all that."

"A speech for English? Why do they have to work *together* on a speech for English?"

Yvonne shrugged.

Heck put his hands on his hips. "Damn fucked-up day."

Dinners with the three of them were frequently tense these days. Tina picked at her food. She had never eaten well, not even as a baby when Yvonne had played games to get her to eat. Now she would eat one or two bites of her dinner and spend the rest of the meal rearranging the food on her plate. Later, she would sneak into the kitchen for ice cream.

"I mailed the package to Edward," Yvonne said. "Took my whole lunch hour, getting over to the post office and waiting in line."

It was a Christmas present for Edward, in Ceylon, things he had especially asked for—disposable razors, deodorant, new underwear, notebook paper, scissors, several boxes of colored chalk. He was teaching in a rural school where the students used chalk and slates instead of paper. Yvonne and Heck had also chosen a couple of short-sleeved shirts, several paperback novels, and a big bag of Good 'N Plenty, his favorite candy.

"Thanks," Heck said. "I imagine he'll be glad to see some things from home along about Christmas."

"Katie called me at work," Yvonne said. "I put money in her account."

"What for?"

"She had to pay for some trip the debate team is taking to New York."

"How come she didn't call here? I'd like to talk to her too."

"She says she's busy in the evenings."

"Uh huh."

Tina sighed loudly and put one foot up on the chair, hugged her knee.

Yvonne glared at the knee, and Tina dropped her leg. "I'm going up to study," she said.

"I'd like to find out how *you're* doing," Heck said.

"Doesn't sound like it." Tina looked up at the ceiling, then picked up her fork again to change the shape of the piles on her plate.

"What is that on your ear?" Heck asked.

"I got a few more holes punched."

"Let me see," Yvonne said and turned Tina's chin. "Why'd you do that?"

She had a big gold bangle earring hanging from her lobe. Now there were also eight sparkling earrings going up the edge of one ear. "It's not a big deal. I just did it. I'm thinking about having five or six punched in the other ear."

"Why didn't you ask us?"

"It's my ear."

"You might not want that later on," Yvonne said. "Then you have an earful of ugly holes."

"But it's *my* ear. It's what *I* feel like doing. It's *my* fashion statement."

"It's a fairly permanent statement," said Yvonne.

"Why do you want to make a statement like this anyway?" Heck asked. "You look strange and cheap."

"That's your opinion. You're not thinking about me. You're only thinking about yourself. You want me to look one way.

Just like all the other uptight, 'moving on up,' middle-class niggers."

"You know we don't use that word in this house," Yvonne said.

Tina groaned. "You're missing my point."

"I guess so," Heck said. "Please explain it to us."

"That I want to do what I want to do."

"Yeah, so would we all. However, there are always consequences. And your mother and I are trying to get you to think of the consequences."

"Consequences of looking strange?"

"That's right! We don't look strange, and we don't want you to, either. Even if that makes us uptight and moving on up."

" 'Cause if I look strange I won't get into Wellesley."

"You can go wherever you want. But, as a matter of fact, you won't get into Wellesley or any other school because of your grades."

"I don't want to go there. I'd be strange there just with this color skin."

Yvonne put her hand to her forehead. "What are you getting at, child?"

"I'm not like you, and I don't want to be like you. Just that. Get it?"

Heck enjoyed the midweek gospel sings at church, so he and Yvonne went nearly every Wednesday night. Reverend Talbert generally spoke a few words, mentioned some members of the congregation to be remembered in prayer, and gave the rest of the time over to the choir master to direct the singing of the hymns—"Shall We Gather at the River?" "The Little Brown Church in the Wildwood," "The Old Rugged Cross."

The church was four blocks from their house. In all the

years they had attended, they had only driven to it a handful of times—when Yvonne was just up from childbed, when there was a thunder and lightning storm early one Sunday morning, after Heck's heart surgery. The rest of the times they had pushed strollers when the babies were small, led the older ones by the hand, ambled along in the spring sunshine or winter dustings of snow, proud of their growing, handsome boys and beautiful little girls. Now on Wednesday nights, just he and Yvonne walked the four blocks, hand in hand.

People were gathered inside the doors, in the narrow lobby, out of the cold, not yet ready to sit down. Yvonne was grabbed by Ferne Griffith. They had to make plans about the holiday ornament sale.

Heck made his way through the crowd shaking a few hands, nodding greetings, patting backs. He spotted Arthur Davis, a small dapper man in a blue striped suit, with a pencil-line mustache. Heck was much taller and broader and felt slovenly in the suit he had worn all day, which had lost its shape from too many cleanings.

"Arthur," Heck said and stuck out his hand.

"Oh no. When the principal comes to me I know I've got trouble," said Arthur.

"What's with T-man?" Heck asked, coming straight to the point. "You're his uncle, aren't you?"

Arthur grimaced. "What'd he do this time?"

"Cussed out a teacher the other day. He was pissed off all outta bounds. I suspended him. But he worries me. Who's looking out for him?"

Arthur frowned and shook his head. "I've washed my hands of that child. I've taken him and his brother to ball games and circuses and amusement parks ever since they were little. Their family doesn't have a whole lotta money, so I've done some treating over the years. T-man's mother—that's my sister—was always saying, 'I've got one good son and one bad one,' and now it seems like she was right. He's been in trouble since he was five years old. He's got a mean temper. What you gonna do? All you can tell him is to tone it down, and he don't listen to that anymore."

It was easier, Heck thought, to see through the tangle of knots that other families got themselves into than it was to see a way through the tangle they were in with Tina. It was better to think about T-man. Heck wanted to think about him. It was something concrete he could do. "He's got a bad reputation to live up to, huh?" Heck said. "I've seen lots of boys like that. Some of 'em come out all right. If we can get to him somehow."

"Well, you'll be paddling upstream with this kid. Now he's hanging with an uncle on his father's side. They're all bad on that side. Man just got acquitted of stealing. He got off on a technicality, but I think he was guilty. T-man has just naturally gravitated to him."

"Teachers don't think he's such a bad kid. Only he's got a short fuse."

"He's big and rough."

Heck looked down at Arthur. "Nothing wrong with being big. Your sister big?"

Arthur snapped his fingers. " 'Bout like that. She said she never understood where this child came from."

"I'll tell you what. You send her in to me. Gotta come in anyway to get him off suspension."

"She probably doesn't even know he's been suspended."

"Send her in," Heck persisted. "Maybe we can get some things straightened out."

Arthur shook his head. "I don't know."

"If he shows some small improvement, will you take him

out somewhere again? Movie? Hockey game? Maybe just by himself?"

"Heck, you don't know this boy. He don't know how to act."

"I'd appreciate it if you'd just give him another chance."

Reverend Talbert was calling them to worship. Many people had already filtered in to take their seats. Heck found Yvonne and guided her to a pew. He closed his eyes and let the music wash through him. He sang the familiar, solacing words without paying attention. Instead, he was thinking how, maybe, one good thing would come of this sorry day. He might be able to pull T-man out of that knot. He wondered if he still had the old touch to turn a kid like that around. If he did, then maybe he could hold on a little longer.

But then he remembered Canaletti. Turning a kid or two around didn't count for much anymore. That wouldn't produce good test scores. Besides, there were so many more kids who needed help now. Not even an army could rescue them all. And look, even his own daughter mocked him these days.

Danny

DANNY MITCHELL HATED EVery bit of this part of her day: waking up when her body was pleading for two more hours; rushing through a shower and trying to do something with her hair in a hurry since she had dozed seven minutes too long; mashing tuna salad onto bread for two bag lunches as the stench turned her stomach. Then she had to pull Royce, Jr., out of his cocoon and plow through a list of reminders as he drooped half-awake over a bowl of cold cereal. "You left your science homework in by the computer. I put that note for the gym teacher on top of your notebook. Come right home and start your English reading since you have Scouts tonight."

One of the many smaller guilts she had about the divorce—besides teaching full-time at Grant and not providing a male influence in her thirteen-year-old's life—was the fact that Royce had to eat cold cereal every morning. Danny could hardly bear to glance at the bowl because it had assumed the proportions of a symbol—the symbol of her shortcomings.

She threw her folders and books into her briefcase, put on her shoes, and flung her arm over his shoulders. "You okay, Rolls?" She used his nickname more often than not.

His shaggy blond hair hung over his eyes. "Yeah."

She kissed his forehead. "I love you, sweetheart. But guess what?"

"You're late."

"Right!" Before she closed the front door, she called, "Don't forget your lunch!"

Guy Tomblin waited in his red pickup, the exhaust puffing out like cartoon bull-snorts in the chilly air. It was a brand-new truck in which he often hauled tools or materials to school where he was an aide in the sheet-metal shop. A sticker smack in the middle of the back bumper declared, *I'm the man your mother warned you about.* Danny wondered what people thought of her riding with him. Did they think she was being abducted? Having carpooled with him for two months now, she knew he was harmless.

"Ready for another day of blistering excitement?" he asked as she fiddled with the seat belt.

"Tell me it's Friday," she said.

He pulled off, around the corner. The back of the truck fishtailed on the wet leaves. "Wednesday won't do? Dedicated teacher like you wants the week to be over?"

"Dedication's one thing. Exhaustion's another."

He chuckled. "You're like this every morning."

"I am not."

"And by afternoon nothing will shut you up." He imitated her voice. " 'Those seniors won't do a lick of work, but they're basically sweet kids.' "

"I wouldn't say 'a lick of work.' "

" 'If that Terrence Hot-sex doesn't leave Lucinda Peach-face alone under the stairs I'm going to have Heck kick him out.' "

She tapped her foot and stared out her window, enjoying the banter. "Uh huh, and you've only been there two months, and those kids are under your skin too. Who was it you were telling me about the other day? Some sheet-metal genius," she reminded him.

"Sully."

"That's it. Sully. He's so good at estimating and eyeballing lengths that he finishes his projects in half the time."

Guy raised his chin. "Kid's a genius."

"So you get involved with them too."

"I don't get involved. I just say the kid is good."

"I hope you tell him that."

"Sure. What else am I there for? I tell 'em what they're doing right and what they're doing wrong. I tell 'em when the work is good."

She had to smile. Guy was rough around the edges, but he had the right instincts. Just what the shop boys needed. Heck had been smart in hiring him.

At the first faculty meeting, before school started, she had noticed Guy across the room. With his back to her, she had mistaken him for Royce, her ex.

Guy was square-jawed and blue-eyed handsome. The lines in his face spoke of his having been around. He was better-looking than Royce, and he was certainly easier to talk to. Danny had liked him immediately.

Maybe it was the shock of seeing someone who resembled Royce, yet was so different. Or maybe the time had finally come for her to start looking at men again, after three years of grief and guilt.

They soon discovered that he lived in an apartment not far from her house in suburban Chevy Chase. After twelve years back and forth in the car by herself, she was ready for a carpool partner. Maybe that would lead to something more. Not that she had any specific agendas in mind—she was still very iffy about dating again—but at least she could imagine going out with him. Occasionally in the last two months he had acted interested, but no invitations had been forthcoming, not even a phone call for other than car-pooling logistics.

She watched the buildings and parked cars flash by. Maybe it was just as well. She didn't want to do anything to hurt the relationship with Rolls.

Two police cars were sitting out front when they arrived at school.

"Great! What's this about?" Danny said.

As soon as she got inside she turned toward the office. Guy headed down to the shop. "Aren't you going to come see what the excitement's about?" she called to him across the lobby.

He shrugged. "Doesn't concern me. Why should I?"

She went on to the office where a gaggle of teachers had gathered.

"What happened?" she asked a colleague.

"Someone busted up Heck's office."

She excused herself and went to take a look. Heck and two police officers were standing in the mess, talking. The destruction was awful. Another officer was hunched over the desk scraping at something with a small tool.

She tiptoed across the broken glass. "Attendance problems finally get you down, Heck?"

He didn't smile. "Danny." He motioned for her to come closer. "Don't you and that Tomblin ride in together?"

"Yes."

"Where is he?" Heck asked.

"He went to the shop."

Heck raised his eyebrows to the officers, and they wrote something down.

"Why?" Danny asked.

"Have you heard he's been making comments to girls? Some teachers are aware of it."

"Comments?"

"Obscene comments."

She shook her head. "Not Guy. You're nuts."

Heck nodded. "Yep, and now he's a suspect for this, too."

"Why?"

"Go on, Danny. We'll talk later."

Danny wandered toward the office she had acquired as head of the English department. She had come to Grant as a student teacher from a master's program at Georgetown. White, idealistic, a young mother, she had thought of Grant as a way station toward another school where she would build her career. But the school had captivated her. Heck had had a lot to do with it. He kept the students in line with growls and gruff bellows so that they knew he meant business. But he was also gentle when gentleness was needed. He was a principal who cared, and she liked that.

She had gone to him near the end of her student-teaching stint to ask whether there was any chance she could stay at Grant. He had visited her classroom twice when she was teaching. The first time she was so nervous she had choked on her own spit. The second time was better. He hired her. Since then, over the years, they had become friends.

He regularly drifted down to her office in the afternoons, after most of the teachers, secretaries and staff had gone home. They would talk about Grant, about his kids, her divorce, movies, news events, politics. She was sorry for him now, knowing that he must be feeling pressured and embarrassed by the attack on his office. The police were wanting names, and he had to come up with some. But Guy? Incredible! Obscene with the girls? Never.

Out of a first-period class of twenty-five students, fourteen were present when she got there. These were her bright eleventh-graders. Five who were on the roll had never shown up in September. Another ten came maybe twice a week. She constantly bugged the kids who were present to drag their friends to school. But it made little difference.

"Punctuation exercise on page one-oh-nine," she said. "Five minutes."

They groaned as they always did and she responded in her usual way. "Wake you up. Yes, sir, nothing, like commas and semicolons to give a person thrills first thing in the morning. Like sticking your face under a faucet."

She hated the mechanics—the grammar, capitalization, punctuation. Nothing turned kids off to English or to school faster than mind-numbing rules taught as if they were the pinnacle of all reason and insight. But there were citywide tests based on three hundred pages of leaden curriculum. "Get it out of the way and keep it brief" was her philosophy, so they could go on to the good stuff—poetry, debates, writing that drew on their experiences. She knew mechanics wouldn't hold them in school, but expressing their opinions, arguing about issues, pouring out their feelings on paper might. They were learning, they were reading and writing. But more importantly, it kept them here.

"Glad to see you back, Marcus," she commented as she handed back corrected papers.

He smiled and nodded. "Thank you, Mrs. Mitchell."

"And I *know* you're back to stay."

"Miss you too much when I'm on the outside," he said, and grinned.

"Keep trying for that A," she returned. "Where's Cirri?"

A couple of girls giggled and he threw them a look. Danny prided herself on being a busybody, on keeping as current as she could on the kids' romances. Some of this news she came by through their papers, some just by observing. It surprised and pleased them when she knew. More than a couple of times, they had come to her for advice.

She had been happy to see Marcus and Cirri together for the last week or so. Even though she liked to give him a hard time in class, she thought he was a good kid. He worked hard. Despite his knock-you-out looks and the girls who hovered around him, he wasn't too conceited. If she could keep him in school, she would have accomplished something, because he had the ability to go far. But already he was messing up. Heck had suspended him. They hadn't actually caught him with the drugs, but they might as well have.

That's where she thought Cirri might help, though Cirri had been missing a lot of school lately herself, and Danny wasn't sure why. Cirri was smart and serious, perceptive for her age.

Marcus was good for Cirri, too. Cirri was pretty and graceful and wise, but she had no self-confidence. Danny told Cirri every other time she saw her that she had a good head on very pretty shoulders, but she knew Cirri didn't buy it. Wouldn't she *have* to start buying it if she had won over the eleventh-grade heartthrob, though?

Danny finished passing out the papers and waited, her arms

and ankles crossed, leaning against her desk. They were so young and had so much life in front of them. This early love and testing the boundaries of right and wrong and getting to know themselves seemed, sometimes, silly and innocent. But it wasn't, not for these kids anyway. This was the time when major events could suddenly spin them off in a new direction. Marcus could get caught one more time and be sent to prison. Forget the diploma. He would get a grand education in deceit and dealing. Cirri could get pregnant, quit school, give up on herself entirely.

Danny had started in the business as a liberal, or as her ex, Royce, had called her, a 'flaming asshole liberal.' Now she knew she couldn't save any souls or produce miracles. They had to save themselves if they were going to do it. All she was trying to do was keep them in school and to show them someone cared.

So she repeated her question. "Where's Cirri?"

Marcus shrugged. "How should I know?"

"Why isn't she here?"

"She said she had too much to do."

"You tell her I said she's already pretty enough. She doesn't have to spend any more time getting fixed up for you."

The class yelped and hooted. "Whooee, Marcus! She cut you down, man."

Marcus ducked his head, then raised it at a waggish angle. Danny could tell he was a little peeved. "Anything else I should tell her?"

"Yeah. Tell her she's a lucky girl to have you coming around to see her."

The class went wild again, but this time, because of the compliment, Marcus didn't mind.

Quintina Jasper, Heck's youngest daughter, sat in the back with her feet propped up on the empty chair in front of her, sloppily scribbling the answers to the exercises on neon pink notebook paper that hurt Danny's eyes when she tried to read it. Tina lived up to the reputation that had preceded her. She was completely different from her brothers and sisters, all of whom had also gone through Grant. Tina didn't take school seriously. She was sullen and cocky.

In this class of students who generally did pretty well when they bothered to come to school, she stood out. She did the minimum, didn't try much, didn't seem to care, though it was clear that she had the brains to do fine, if she ever used them. She had been placed in this upper-level group because of Heck. Danny knew how much it was hurting him that she was refusing to work.

Danny tried to treat Tina the same way she treated everyone else, but it was hard. She wanted to shake the girl and say, "Hey, wake up and look at what you're doing to your mother and father! Look at what you're doing to yourself! You are in the unusual position of having opportunities waiting for you. College, connections for jobs, anything you want can be arranged for you because of your father. Not another child in this school has such possibilities available to him or her. Why are you wasting this? Just do a little goddamned work!"

But she didn't dare say this. It would only stiffen Tina's defiance. Instead she made teasing, challenging, friendly comments the way she did with the other kids—to build rapport, to keep things light and moving along, to open up channels of trust that she hoped she could lead the kids through later in the year.

Danny wandered toward the back of the room, reading over shoulders, urging them on through the exercise, stopping to help if they were stuck.

"Tina, I wish you would get some brighter paper," she said.

"I depend on you to jolt me when I'm correcting. This pink is so boring."

"I'll see what I can do," Tina muttered.

Danny leaned on Tina's desk. "Just a little hint. Could be you had more of the answers right on last week's test. But I couldn't tell. I couldn't read the handwriting. Is there any way you might take a little more care with it?"

Tina closed her eyelids and opened them again slowly, indicating that this was so boring she was about to fall asleep. "I don't think so."

Danny straightened and continued her stroll. "Up to you."

"Maybe she thinks what we're doing in here ain't worth the trouble," Nick Tiebault said.

Tina shrugged one shoulder. Impossible to know if she agreed or disagreed. But it didn't matter anyway. This was Nick's standard line. Danny had been unfortunate enough to have gotten him in class two years in a row. He was aggressive and challenging, hostile with nearly everyone.

"I mean, really," he went on, "this stuff sucks." He gestured to the book in front of him. "And the reading we do has no point. Or if it does, you beat it to death."

"Lucky you to be able to benefit from my expert teaching two years in a row, huh, Nick? I guess we were just meant for each other," said Danny.

"Yeah, in somebody's nightmare."

She had to hand it to him. He was quick.

"I could probably show porno flicks in here, and you'd think they were boring," she shot back.

"Yeah, I would." He leaned back and grinned. " 'Cause I seen most of 'em already."

The class exploded. "Go on, Nick! Yeah!"

Danny suspected that a lot of Nick's behavior came from the fact that he was white. The handful of whites at Grant had a tough time of it. There were only so many ways a kid in the minority could gain some respect. Nick had chosen to play the role of being the baddest thing around: hassle the teachers; push the limits of what was acceptable language, dress and behavior; brag about exploits; drop hints about the wild life; keep a step ahead of the other kids; be unpredictable. His approach worked. He twirled the diamond stud in his ear, wore the pointy little black shoes and was accepted by the kids. The teachers all thought he was a pain in the ass.

But Danny also had a reputation to maintain. She could spar with any kid and make it come out all right in the end. "What's your favorite porno flick?" she asked.

He laughed. "You really want to know?"

"I asked, didn't I?"

" 'Teacher's Titties,' " he answered.

The kids went crazy again. Danny started collecting their papers, not saying a word, letting him bask for a moment.

She knew they were waiting for her comeback. "You're right," she said. "That does sound boring."

The class howled.

She picked up the novel they were reading and said, "Page one eighty-nine. Enough chills and goose bumps for one day."

Mid-morning, Danny hurried through the halls, craving coffee, hoping that some Good Samaritan had brought in Danish or donuts, leftover Halloween candy, anything. It was her drive for mid-morning sweets that kept her ten pounds heavier than she would have liked.

Anya Cooper, another white student, fell in step with her, "I got no sleep last night," the girl said.

This was Anya's code, her way of letting Danny know that her parents were at each other again. It had been going on for as long as Anya could remember, she'd told Danny. Last year, as a tenth grader, Anya had regularly slept through Danny's class. Eventually, she had confided in Danny that her parents spent half their lives beating each other up, and the other half mooning and cooing at each other. At one PTA meeting Mrs. Cooper's wrist was in a fresh cast. Mr. Cooper sported an eggplant-colored eye. Yet they pawed each other through the meeting as if they were teenagers in the back row of a dark movie theater.

Anya was the oldest of six kids—six reconciliations, as Danny thought of them. The girl was unkempt and uncared for. Her hair hung in greasy blond strands. Scars from pimples had already etched her cheeks. Her clothes were too small and inappropriate for the season.

Last year Danny had made some efforts to help the girl. For Christmas she had slipped Anya a shoebox present of shampoo, conditioner, a fancy bar of soap, a package of barrettes, deodorant, and a pamphlet on teenage hygiene habits she'd gotten from the nurse.

The other kids in school made comments about BO and blackheads when Anya was around. Danny hoped her none-too-subtle gift might help. But she never saw any evidence of Anya's using any of the products. The only effect it had was to cause Anya to latch on to Danny. Anya assumed she was a favorite, that Danny liked to have her around, and wanted to know all the details of her life.

Eventually, it came out that Mrs. Cooper had confiscated the shoebox's contents in order to adorn herself for Mr. Cooper. And Anya didn't mind because as long as her parents were being devoted to each other, Anya and her brothers and sisters could sleep.

Danny didn't have Anya in class this year, but Anya had memorized Danny's schedule. She knew just where to intercept her in the halls and was a master at communicating a dump truck of information in the briefest of sentences.

"She bit my dad's ear and he bit her back. Bit her nose. Then he was up all night yelling. 'You must want me to be a goddamn one-ear Michelangelo, goddamn cunt. What you want? A artist?'"

Danny shook her head as they threaded through the crush in the halls. Mr. and Mrs. Cooper's stunts were dramatic and useful for a girl who needed to squeeze out some attention from somebody.

Last year Danny had quizzed Anya about how far the violence went. Did they ever hit her or any of her siblings, ever punish them in a bad way? Was she afraid of her parents? But the answers were always reassuring, at least as far as the kids went. Anya wasn't clean, but she wasn't starving. She couldn't sleep when her parents fought, but she didn't seem emotionally scarred. Both parents were in the home, however strange a home it was. The family was intact, which was more than could be said of Danny's own home. So she simply listened and occasionally asked questions.

"How's your mom's nose?"

"All swollen up. She says she should get rabies shots the way my Dad foams at the mouth. And she says she's leaving."

Danny stopped at the door of the teacher's lounge. "What do you think?"

"I think they're really mad at each other this time. I don't think they're going to make up."

Danny sighed and put her fingertips on the girl's shoulders. "You think that every time."

Anya screwed up her face. "Yeah, but they were really mean to each other last night."

"Meaner than when your mom's wrist got broken?"

"Oh yeah. That time, soon as my dad heard it pop, he fell down on his knees and begged her to forgive him. His eye was about swollen shut from where she'd hit him, but he did it. Then they cried and he took her to the emergency room. Last night ... I don't know. They still want to fight some more."

The late bell rang.

"Write me a pass?" Anya asked.

Danny held out a hand into which Anya slapped a scrap of paper and a pencil. Danny scrawled the excuse, then pushed into the lounge, dying for five hundred empty calories.

Forty years ago the faculty lounge had been a home ec room. The yellow ruffled curtains printed with copper tea kettles remained, an odd reminder of 1950s cheeriness. This was in contrast to the group of teachers who sat around smoking and slapdashing red marks across student papers. They were a hardened, cynical crew who had been teaching too long and maybe had no feel for it in the first place. The lounge intermission was the best part of their day, when they didn't have to be "baby-sitting the bastards."

Sure, everybody had bad days and needed to escape from the teenage hordes. But this group competed with each other for who could hate Grant High the most. For the sake of camaraderie, Danny listened and sometimes joined in their complaints.

"What can Jasper do? It's really in the cops' hands at this point, till they analyze the evidence."

"What evidence do you need? It was a kid. Most likely someone he's suspended in the last coupla days."

"My bet is it was Marcus Chance."

Danny poured coffee into a foam cup, dumped in creamer and sugar. In the center of the table was a cinnamon-pecan coffee ring topped with icing.

"Marcus Chump. Why the hell doesn't Heck throw those bums out? Marcus and about fifty other kids."

Danny reached between the speakers for a piece of the coffee cake.

These two—Samuels in history and Shunks in math—had a crusade going against certain boys. Those kids weren't here to learn, the teachers griped. They were only here to socialize and sell dope. And Heck was too lenient with them. She'd heard it before.

"Danny, it's going to make you fat," Shunks, whom the kids called Skunks, warned her.

"No more than it will you," she said.

The irony was that neither of them taught much anyway. History with Samuels was basically an audio-visual course. He showed movies; the kids talked. He had tenure and a used-car business. His income from sales was double what he earned teaching.

Skunks, the kids said, spent the periods with his back to the class, solving problems on the board. He didn't care what they did with their time as long as they were halfway quiet.

"Heck's got to have proof before he goes throwing anybody out," Ginger Hartley said. An art teacher, she was one voice of reason in the room.

"He'll have proof. Cops are in there fingerprinting, shoeprinting, the works," Samuels said.

"I don't mean for just that. I mean for other stuff. You say those boys are troublemakers. What have they done?"

"Didn't T-man cuss you out coupla days ago?"

"T-man. There's another one," Skunks put in.

"And Heck suspended him," Danny said in Heck and Ginger's defense.

"He'll be back," Skunks grumbled. "Maybe he already has been. To fuck up Jasper's office."

"He's a mixed-up kid," Ginger said.

"Listen at you now," Skunks said. "Two days ago you were ready to kill the little fucker."

"He's not my favorite person in the world. I hate to see his name come up on my class list, but to be professional . . ."

Samuels laughed. "Professional baby-sitters. Keep 'em here till they graduate to Lorton. Why?"

Kitty Harmer, typing teacher, looked up from her magazine. " 'Cause we love our jobs."

"I know you love it, Kitty," Skunks said.

She winked. "Payday, sweetheart."

Danny reached in for a smaller piece of coffee cake.

"God, Danny." Skunks smirked.

"Shut up," she said. "Let me get fat in peace."

She went to the office to pick up her mail and found a message to call Rolls's gym teacher.

The office was busy. The janitor was cleaning Heck's room: the steady swoosh of the broom, then the sound of the glass as it hit the bottom of a metal garbage can. A lineup of kids sat on the hot seats, waiting to be seen by Heck. The secretaries and assistant principal seemed devoted to their work this morning, eager to prove their worth in the crisis.

Danny stretched the cord of the one available phone as far as it would go and got ahold of the gym teacher.

"You know I take these excuses with a grain of salt," he said. "Royce never seems as sick or as hurt as you make out in the notes. Is there some problem with gym class?"

No problem, except that the kid was small for his age, he hated undressing in front of others, and she wrote these lame-brained excuses for him pretty regularly just to make his day a little easier.

"It's not his favorite class," Danny said. "He complains

about undressing. And he has some asthmatic tendencies when he's been running hard."

"Needs to build up his endurance."

She rubbed her forehead and stared absently at the police cars parked out front. "Yes. I guess so. He's just so small. I think he feels he can't keep up."

"Well, he can't keep up, it's true, when he's sitting out all the time. And he's not so small. Lotta kids haven't gone through their growth spurts yet."

Knowing he was right, she asked, "What would you suggest?"

"He can do it. No more excuses."

She took a deep breath, wondering how she was going to explain this to Rolls. "Okay."

The voice on the other end grew friendlier. "He's a fine kid. Don't worry about him so much."

It was the line meant to reassure parents after a touchy phone call, pointing up inadequacies. She used it herself all the time.

She didn't feel reassured. Sure he was a fine kid—quiet, shy, serious. A mildly depressed kid, who didn't think too highly of himself and didn't like exposing himself to the rough-and-tumble of basketball or wrestling or soccer. He said he didn't like charging in after a ball knowing he was going to get kicked or punched.

She couldn't blame him. She'd never been big on gym when she was his age. Even now the national mania over exercise left her uninspired. Plus, this was one way she could lighten his burden. Maybe it wasn't a hot breakfast, but she could jot a note that assured him a break once or twice a week.

On the other hand, there was the issue of maleness. Weren't boys supposed to love the physical, the sweat and guts of competition? Maybe by giving in to these requests for excuses, she was making him too feminine.

She liked Rolls's sensitivity and his quiet ways. She could be plenty aggressive and tough when she needed to be. But beyond the stereotypes, she just worried about the imbalance of growing up with one parent. And so it come back to the divorce. He had no dad. Royce, Sr., had moved to New Orleans. There was no regular male influence in Rolls's life. She hoped he'd be able to compensate for it in some way eventually. But for now, the gym teacher was right. She should stop with the notes.

Nick Tiebault strolled into her office, rolling on the balls of his feet as always, a notebook hanging from one arm. "So when you bringing in the porno flicks? I wanna sell tickets."

Danny left her door open during the lunch period to encourage kids to come in. Most knew the limits, knew not to abuse this privilege and her patience. Just at that moment she was trying to finish some evaluations that had to be downtown today. Interoffice mail left at one. She had fifteen minutes. "I thought we were finished with that little joke."

"Maybe so. Flicks would be better than what we're doing, though."

"Gimme a break."

He threw a leg over a chair and sat down facing her desk. His diamond earring flashed. "Miz Brown's at it again. She's preaching racism in that class, and that's not right."

This was not a new complaint. "Can we talk about it some other time, Nick?" Danny gestured to the papers. "I've got . . ."

"Today she made us chant some African thing about blackness is wholeness or some shit. And she has all these supposedly inspirational proverbs she says all the time, like, 'The young antelope that loses her path ends up lining the drum with her skin.' Now that's gruesome. I don't wanna study all that crap."

Nick's attitude was bad, but he was a good student. He did the work, handed it in on time, and mostly aced the tests. Once, last year, she had asked him about it. "How do you do this, Nick? Your parents on your back or something?"

"Foster parents, you mean. Don't give a damn. But I wanna get outta this shithole fast as I can."

She respected his determination.

"Can't you get me transferred outta there? I swear I'm gonna smack her the next time she says that whitey is the curse of the earth."

"What can I do? She's in the history department. And why do you come to me, after all that crap you were giving me in class today?"

"I can't help it if your class is boring. I gotta say what I think. But I thought you had some power in this school. And you're white. You should understand." He jabbed a finger at her. "You gotta let people know she's encouraging violence."

"She's been teaching like that for years," Danny explained, wishing he would leave. "You just have to live with it. And I've got to work, so get out of here."

He smirked at her and tipped back his chair. "I think she's a lezzie."

"Did I ever tell you I'm glad you're going to be a senior next year?"

"Maybe it was some white kids who trashed Dr. Jasper's office. Did you ever think of that? Kid's who're fed up with Miz Brown, and black *folk* in general."

Danny raised her eyes tiredly. "Is this a confession?"

He laughed. "I think they were looking for drugs in Jasper's office. Don't you think he deals?"

"Go away."

"No shit. There is some serious dealing going on at this school. And most everybody looks the other way. Why is that?"

"The door is that way. Please close it on your way out."

He got up and sauntered across the room. "You don't want to hear about it 'cause you and Jasper are bosom buddies. I've seen you in here after school. But I'll tell you something. Nobody knows who all's dealing in this school. He looks the other way. And you wouldn't *think* of criticizing him. The two of you got something going?"

She pointed with a straight arm. "Out!"

She never got a chance to talk to Heck. When she went to see him after school, he had already left for the day. "Downtown," the secretary said.

Guy was waiting in his truck. The bumper sticker reminded her of what Heck had told her in the morning. She would tell Guy that it might be a good idea to take it off.

He had one cowboy boot up on the dashboard and his head thrown back, listening to the tape of country-western songs she couldn't stand. As soon as she opened the door, he ejected the tape. Then he sat up in slow motion and reached for the key. She'd never seen him so tired.

"Someday," she said.

He started the truck. "Yeah. I got canned."

"They can't fire you!" she said, turning to see his face.

"Oh yes they can." He backed up and pulled out onto the street.

"On what grounds?"

"That I was saying naughty things to the little ladies."

"Did you?"

He shot her a glance. "I just said I did, didn't I?"

"What did you say?"

" 'You got a nice little ass.' 'Keep your buns warm.' That kind of thing."

"For Christ's sake!" She ran her hand up through her hair. "*Why* did you do that?"

He shrugged as he drove. "I've been saying things like that to women all my life."

"Those are girls. And with that stupid bumper sticker, I'm not surprised the kids were upset. Or that you got fired."

"What's wrong with the bumper sticker?"

"You're advertising that you're a lech?"

"I just thought it was funny."

"Jesus Christ. Here I was worrying half the day 'cause my kid doesn't have a male influence in his life."

He drove in silence and steered with one hand. When he wasn't shifting, he rubbed the other hand nervously up and down his thigh in slow motion.

"When did you get the word?" she asked quietly.

" 'Bout eleven."

"Eleven! Why did you wait around?"

"Couldn't leave you there without a lift."

"Guy . . ."

"I screwed up," he said. "I see that. I just didn't think."

"With all these sexual abuse and assault cases smeared all over the papers, you just don't talk to kids that way. Or to anyone for that matter. Not in a school. Even if you don't mean anything."

"This was my first time in a school. On all my other jobs you whistled at the ladies and talked about getting laid. Fights the boredom, talking like that. It just came naturally."

"Why do you want to work in a school anyway? Wouldn't you make a lot more money in those other jobs?"

"Yeah, it was a stupid idea, but once I got my high school

equivalency and some college credit, I figured I'd try something else for a change. At my age, painting cars is not a big thrill anymore."

She'd wondered how old he was, but had never had the opening to ask. "How old are you?"

"Forty-one."

She was thirty-eight. Close enough, she thought, as she watched him change lanes and speed up on an uncongested stretch of road.

"I always hated school," he went on. "Hated the teachers 'cause it seemed like they hated the kids. I thought it'd be fun to see if I could do it different."

She smiled. "I bet the boys in the shop loved your comments."

"Oh yeah. They ate 'em up. Which is partly why I did it, I guess, even though I knew Jasper was having me watched."

"How'd you know?"

"There was a squealer in the class. I knew who he was."

He turned onto her street and pulled up to the curb in front of her house. She needed to say good-bye. He needed to say something about her having to finish out his week of driving. They'd try to make it light and then go their separate ways.

But neither of them said anything for a long moment. She was drawn to him more than before. She felt sorry for him; he'd been out of his element. She was touched that he'd waited for her all day.

"Come on in," she said quietly. "Have a drink or something. The place is a mess, but . . ."

"You're a nice lady. But no thanks."

Then she was afraid he would go. "I'm not just being nice."

He looked past her at the house. "Guess I don't really want to go to my place yet."

She got out and hurried through the last of the fallen leaves, wondering what Rolls was up to, how he'd react to this surprise. She assumed Guy was behind her, but when she turned around he was still back at the truck, tearing off the bumper sticker.

She clicked on the light, dumped her briefcase, and scurried around the living room, picking up newspapers, sneakers, a pizza box, mail, clothes and Rolls's portable phone. Of course, the rug needed vacuuming, and the pillows on the couch were askew. She attempted to ignore what she couldn't immediately fix.

When he came in, she led the way to the kitchen, knowing the mess in there was even worse. She turned on the light over the dirty breakfast dishes and chairs scattered at odd angles to the table. "Scotch, gin, vodka? Bar's open."

"No thanks," he said, looking around the room.

"Beer?"

"I don't drink."

The tension of having a man in the house—this man whom she'd been interested in all these weeks—and the shame of the filth in which she existed made her giddy. He didn't drink, but she was dying for one.

"Why not?"

"I used to drink too much. So I quit."

Alcohol was the cushion that she eased herself down on each evening. It helped her to feel sociable with Rolls and not see him as just one more kid needing attention. It made her relax, which she wouldn't otherwise do. It loosened up her creativity, so that sometimes brilliant ways of presenting new material came to her. At least they seemed brilliant in the evenings.

"Mind if I have one?" she asked.

He shrugged. "It's your house."

"How 'bout a Diet Coke?"

"Fine."

She shoved the dirty dishes away and handed him his Coke. Then she cranked open the gin bottle. When she sat down she saw Rolls's note on the table. He was at a neighbor's house playing Nintendo.

She lifted the note. "My son," she said. "It's hard trying to be everything to everybody. Harriet Housewife I'm not."

He tried a smile but it flickered out. He stared into his glass which he held between his widespread knees, sitting back from the table.

She gave up worrying about her embarrassment. He didn't seem to notice the mess anyway. "What're you going to do now?" she asked.

"Get another job."

"Well, that shouldn't be too hard with your background. I mean, if you're not wanting to get into the school scene again."

He halfway smiled. "My background?"

"Sure. You must have a lot of experience."

"I do," he said. "But I doubt they'd let me go back to work in an auto-body shop. Least, not right away. The program's really strict."

She had gulped down half her drink and thought maybe it had already affected her attention. She had missed something. "Program?"

He sat forward and rested his forearms on the table. "The early release program. I'm an ex-con. And you're Danny Do-gooder, right? Carpool with the guy. Make sure he gets back and forth to school."

She finished her drink, keeping her eyes on him.

"You're going to get ripped," he said.

"I don't know what you're talking about."

"Come on. You're buddy-buddy with Jasper. It's an experimental program. He agreed to take me on."

"What's the experiment?"

"Putting guys like me into jobs they normally wouldn't be able to get, like working in a school." He circled his hands around the Coke on the table without touching the glass. "So since I've fucked up, I've fucked up for a lot of people. Lot of people who believed in the program." He closed his eyes and sighed. "That's what really gets me. I'm so stupid."

"What did you do to get . . ."

"Get put away?"

She nodded.

"Credit-card fraud. Pretty good, huh? Me, a blue-collar guy with a white-collar crime."

"I don't understand."

"When customers paid for repairs at the shops with a card, I'd use their numbers. Now they have more safeguards against that kind of thing. But then, hey, I made a lot of money. It was easy. People trusted me. I've got an honest face."

"How long?"

"Three and a half years of a ten-year sentence. I'm on parole, in a subsidized apartment, in the program. And I probably just blew it all."

His fingernails were neatly trimmed and clean. The muscle in his jaw flexed as he lifted the glass and set it back down again without taking a drink. He looked up at her with innocent blue eyes. The lines in his face held more meaning now. She didn't think he was stupid. His past intrigued her. He *did* have an honest face.

But then she had second thoughts. Could she trust him? She got up and fixed herself another drink.

"Want me to go?"

"No!" she said too fast.

He snorted. "Alone with an ex-con who has been sexually assaulting the delicate ears of young ladies, and who was grilled by cops all day about trashing the principal's office. You should be scared."

She decided to trust him. "Well, I'm not," she said, more slowly this time.

"Why're you on your second drink after only ten minutes, then?"

"I always drink this much."

"It's bad for your health."

She laughed at the absurdity of his concern. "Sure. I know."

Their eyes met and locked. She crossed her arms and leaned on the table. "The police think you did that to Heck's office?"

He turned his face away, pained and angry. "They don't know who the fuck they're looking for. I think they grilled me because I been through it before. Make their jobs easier to talk to someone who's used to an interrogation. Hell, why would I want to trash his office?"

"Who do you think did it?"

"How am I supposed to know? I don't know what he's got on his plate or who hates him or what's in that office that someone might've wanted. Burns me up. Could've been a hundred people. But they come running at me because I got a past."

"And because you were complimenting the girls on their nice behinds."

"Aw, hell."

"Well, at least you don't have to worry about Heck's office anymore. That's over."

"Calm down, in other words."

She lifted a shoulder. "You've got other things to worry about, I guess."

"Just as well, really. I need more money than I was making there. Teachers make lousy money, don't they?"

Their eyes met again, lingered.

"Those truck payments are killing me. And I can only stay in my place till June. Then I'm supposed to move on and let some other lucky bastard have it. A regular place will cost double this one."

"Maybe construction . . ." she began.

"Ductwork. It's simpleminded, but it pays."

They were quiet then, both staring at his Coke. Eventually, he stopped fooling with the glass and slapped his knees. "Gotta go."

She didn't dispute this because she had to round up Rolls, get him his supper and drive him to Scouts. She had three classes' worth of papers to grade.

She followed him to the front door, asking herself if this was going to be good-bye. Did she want it to be, was there anything she could do about it, what did those looks mean, was he really trustworthy?

He stopped and zipped up his jacket halfway. "So, if you weren't just doing a good deed, why'd you come up to me that first day?"

She looked at the floor and decided to answer honestly. "I liked your looks."

He took that in and shook his head. "All this time I thought I could never have a chance with you because you knew about me." He rubbed the back of his neck. "Well, now you do know and I probably really don't have a chance."

"All this time I thought you weren't interested because I didn't like country-western music."

"Well, that *is* a problem."

They smiled at each other. In his smile she detected something new: approval of her, and interest.

"Would you mind if I called you sometime?" he asked.

"That would be fine."

"I promise I won't talk dirty to you."

She smiled and shrugged. She wouldn't mind hearing that
she had a nice ass.

Cirri

MARCUS TOOK CIRRI, PEA AND Willie to teen night. They rode one bus, huddled against a building to wait for the transfer bus, then walked two blocks to the rec department's redbrick building. He had given Cirri his coat, so he hopped and high-jinxed to keep warm. He slipped his arms around her inside the coat, and she hugged him back.

"I got to get you a coat, baby, or I'm gonna freeze to death," he said.

Willie and Pea thought it was funny.

"Why are you dragging us all over town for?" Cirri wanted to know.

"Terms of my 'probation,' as Jasper called it."

"What?"

"Dr. Jasper said I had to make it over here at least once a week and get my grades up. He's just trying to give me something to do with my time so I won't be tempted to be involved in business. There's somebody over here supposed to be checking that I come. I'll do it. I can fool Jasper."

Cirri shook her head. "You're crazy."

There wasn't much happening when they got there. The bare wooden floor echoed as they walked across the big drafty room. Two boys were playing Ping-Pong and several others were leaning against the walls, grunting at good shots, waiting for their turns. Four or five girls were dancing to a rap tape. A couple of little kids, Pea's and Willie's ages, were working on a big jigsaw puzzle on the floor.

"Go play with them kids," Cirri said.

Marcus angled off to watch the Ping-Pong. Cirri, standing alone in Marcus's oversized coat, felt dumb. She didn't want to be out on this cold night. She didn't want to be here having to watch Pea and Willie when it was so much easier at home, in front of the TV or playing with the new kitten. But most of all, she didn't want to be with Marcus this way—with him off across the room and her standing in the middle of the floor with a bunch of strangers.

A man walked past her lugging a case of Cokes. "There's some potato chips in the office. Would you mind bringing them in?" he said. Cirri watched him put the Cokes on the table next to the music and went to get the chips.

In his office was an eight-foot-high poster of Kareem Abdul-Jabar that read, Just Say No. There was also a big schedule of teen night events. A Thanksgiving dinner was planned, a Saturday trip to the Capital Center to see some group, a Christmas dance, a basketball tournament. She grabbed a bag of potato chips and wandered back into the big room.

"You think with all these hogs around, that one little bag is gonna be enough?" the man asked her.

The girls snickered. Marcus was sassing the winner at Ping-Pong, challenging him to a game. It was clear that, as always, he was already making friends. Cirri put the bag on the table and shrugged.

The man threw his arm around Cirri's shoulder and turned her around. "Come on. We'll go get some more. My name's Mr. Van Caspel. The kids call me Van. Hell of a cold night and I can't get it much warmer in here. The old furnace won't do it. But pretty soon you'll be able to take off his coat, I bet. Get some dancing going. They your brother and sister?"

She nodded.

"They're welcome if that's the only way you're able to come. But you're responsible for them even when you're having fun. What's your name?"

"Cirri."

He smiled. "Pretty name for a pretty girl."

He handed her three more bags of chips. His face was round and his head was bald. He looked like a brown bowling ball. And she didn't like him. She didn't like someone talking about all her business like that. "His coat" and "your brother and sister." She took the chips and sauntered back to the table.

More kids had arrived. The music was turned up. A crowd ringed the Ping-Pong table. She leaned against the wall, snug in Marcus's coat, and watched him move.

Marcus was quick and agile. The other boy couldn't get the ball past him. She watched his hands as he cradled the ball before the serve and touched his left hand to the paddle before he swatted the ball back across the net. His hands were delicate, his fingers long and slender. The back of his hand was smooth.

Everyone else saw him bouncing on the balls of his feet, saw him reach nearly all the way under the table with his paddle to get the ball that had curved away from him, and slap it back to his opponent. They saw him grinning to make the other boy nervous, heard him compliment the boy's good shots. They heard his good-natured laugh and knew he was having a fine time. That made them have a fine time too.

But only she noticed his fingers and his hands. Those fingers that had tenderly touched her lips last night, that had encompassed her chin and cheeks while he kissed her, that had fluttered across her belly, making her sweet and swimmy with wanting him.

How was it that she could want him so much, and he could want this? This awful place, the cold, the long ride, the stupid potato chips. Van was watching the match now at the edge of the circle. Music was pounding. Each point made the audience cheer. Cirri knew that Marcus liked this, needed it. He didn't love her, not in any way like she loved him. Thea was right. Marcus Chance would play with some other girl next month. And where would Cirri be then? That was why she couldn't be good to Marcus, why strange, mad words came out of her mouth. Because she knew she had to keep her distance, and that she'd be mad at him one day. Why not now?

She drifted away from the table, even though game point was coming up, and went to see how the kids were. They were starting to argue about the puzzle, so she took them in hand and pulled them over to the table. "Eat. Then we're going," she said. Only trouble was she didn't have the bus fare. She tried to think how she could borrow some.

The match concluded with a wave of cheers and whooping and new challenges for Marcus. Van and Marcus seemed to hit it off. Van was clapping him on the back. Marcus was talking and pointing and grinning as if someone had just handed him the winning lottery ticket.

Cirri looked around and tried to assess who she might ask for the money.

One girl had painted gold highlights in her hair. She wore tight pants and black boots with gold buttons. Cirri was sure she would attract Marcus's attention. For that reason alone, Cirri didn't mind taking money from her. Besides, with all that finery, she looked like she'd have some change in her pocket. Cirri caught her pulling a Coke out of the case. "Could I borrow a dollar? Gotta get these kids home to bed."

But even as the girl wiggled her hand down in those tight pants, Cirri felt low and trifling to be asking for money from a complete stranger. The girl came up with the money and Cirri thanked her.

She herded Pea and Willie to the door, took off Marcus's coat and hung it on a hook where he'd be sure to find it, then left. She was cold immediately. And as she half jogged with the kids at her sides, she realized that this was not a good neighborhood. She hadn't noticed it before because Marcus had been with them. Whenever he was around her senses were half-clouded-over. But now she was aware of the men in the shadows, of the group of boys up ahead under the street light, who appeared to be drunk or stoned or both. She saw now that there weren't any houses along here—just stores with iron gates closed down over their doors—a liquor store, a palm reader's, a discount shoe store.

She crossed the street before they got too close to the group of boys and hurried toward the bus stop. This side of the street was darker and the boys' laughter bounced off the buildings. She thought they were laughing at her, at her vulnerability, walking out here at night with these two little kids and only a dollar and a few pennies. The bus stop was halfway up the next block. Then she'd have to stop and watch them out of the corner of her eye, because what was to keep them from coming for her?

She was being crazy, she told herself. They were having a

good time right where they were. Why would they want to bother her? In her own neighborhood she wasn't afraid. She knew which corners to avoid, which doorways always had someone waiting with a ready deal. But here everything was new. If she acted like she didn't give a damn about them, they probably wouldn't give a damn about her.

She put a hand on Pea's shoulder and one on Willie's, pulled them in close to her, talked like they were just passing the time of day.

"I'm cold," Pea whined.

"Well, we're going home. Be there in a little while."

"I hope Furry's not cold," Willie said.

"Law, Furry's been curled up sleepin', I bet, since the minute we left. He be nice and warm."

"How come Marcus didn't come home with us?" Pea wanted to know.

"You saw him playing his Ping-Pong. He wanted to stay and do that."

"Uh huh. You just left him," Willie said. "Didn't even tell him 'bye."

"What's that got to do with you, Willie James, huh?"

"You could've used his coat," Pea said.

"Then he would be cold, wouldn't he?"

"Hey, little mother!" one of the boys in the group shouted. "Come on over here. We havin' a party."

Cirri kept up the pace, pushing Pea and Willie along. The bus stop was right ahead, but that wasn't any consolation since no bus was coming.

"Party wid us a little bit, then my man'll *drive* you home!"

Cirri ignored them and reached the stop. She stood with her back to the group, listening for any movements. She put her hand in her pocket, gripped her house key. She could hurt somebody with it, she knew.

"We offering her a party and she don't even care."

" 'Course she don't care 'bout you. She ain't got a close look at your face yet. Come look at this man. He look just like Sugar Ray Leonard."

"Got some nice moves, too, baby."

If talk was all they were going to do, she could handle it. Her teeth were chattering with the cold, and she knew the kids felt her tension because they were still now. But she was fine. She could hold on.

Then she heard running. There was no bus, no friendly-looking place ahead. She whirled, bared her teeth, and held the key like a knife ready to strike at eyes or a cheek.

It was Marcus with his coat hanging open, his chest heaving, eyes watering with the cold. "What the fuck you doin'?" he demanded. "Why'd you leave? I got to be chasin' you every minute of the day and night? This is a bad part of town."

She glanced over his shoulder at the boys under the street-light. They hadn't moved. A couple of them were watching Marcus.

"Goddammit, Cirri. Why you so skittish?"

She dropped her hand, slid the key back into her pocket.

"If you don't want to have nothing to do with me, then tell me. Don't leave me there looking like a goddamned fool."

"I was the fool to come with you."

"I thought you'd like it."

"Well, I didn't!"

He walked a couple of steps away from her, caught his breath, then came back and sloughed off his coat. "Put this on."

"I don't need it."

"Quit being so stuck up and put this on!"

She took the coat and slipped it on but didn't close it.

"You act like you don't need nobody. You can handle any ol'

thing, right? Well, I don't want somebody like that. I like it when people need me, and laugh at what I say, and I can do for them. And if we gonna have something together, then you gotta relax your guard some."

She wanted to cry because she felt that she had lost him already. He didn't love her. He didn't even like her. She was too stuck up. And tomorrow or the next day he'd find someone easier, someone who'd give him everything he wanted. But she didn't say anything. If she opened her mouth she knew she'd cry. So she just stood in silence. The quiet between them was hostile and hopeless. Finally, the bus came.

As usual, Mama wasn't home when they got to the apartment. The kids ran in to find the kitten. Marcus and Cirri stood at the door.

"I won't come in unless you want me to," he mumbled.

She nodded, still unable to talk.

He lifted her chin with his fingers. "You want me to?" he asked gently. His eyes were kind, apologetic.

"Yes," she whispered and the tears came.

They held each other, exchanging warmth. Her tears wouldn't stop. He held on and stroked her hair, kissed her forehead, patted her back. "Yeah, baby, go 'head," he murmured.

She wasn't sure why she was crying so much or why she couldn't stop, but she knew she felt better now. The coil of tension in her was gradually unwinding. She felt weak with happiness. Marcus was holding her up, kissing her, caring about her, and that was fine.

They closed the door to the apartment and stood in the dark kitchen, still kissing, running their hands up and down each other's bodies.

She didn't care, right then, if Marcus was going to leave her tomorrow or next week. Tonight it seemed that he would stay long enough.

Only one thing, like a bad bruise on a perfect apple, bothered her: Mama was somewhere out in all that cold.

The next morning, after Pea and Willie and Marcus left for school and Mama came home to sleep, the policeman knocked on the door.

"Cirrus James?" he asked and showed his badge.

She was instantly afraid. "Yes."

"I have a few questions. Can I come in?"

"What about?"

"Marcus Chance."

She was worried, but she knew she could lie well enough to fool him, and besides, Marcus wasn't here. If the cop had wanted to talk about Mama, she couldn't have let him in.

He glanced around the room—at the pillows and blanket on the couch where the kids slept, at the TV sitting on the old card table, at the closed door to Mama's bedroom.

"Where were you last Tuesday evening, Miss James?" he asked.

She fought her fear. "Tuesday?"

He took out a notebook. "Three nights ago."

"We got Kentucky Fried Chicken and came back here to eat it," she told him, wondering if her voice sounded shaky.

"Who?"

"Marcus and my brother and sister and me."

"Then what?"

Tuesday had been her first night with Marcus. She didn't want to talk about it. "We went to sleep."

"Marcus, too?"

She nodded.

"What time was that?"

"We got the chicken 'round 'bout seven-thirty . . ."

"And you came straight back here?"

"Yes."

"Was Marcus with you the whole time?"

Mama opened the door, put a hand to her head. "What's this fuss?" She squinted. "You done somethin', Cirri?"

"Are you Mrs. James?" the policeman asked.

"Why're you here?" Mama demanded.

"There was some vandalism up at the high school, Mrs. James," he said. "I'm checking on the whereabouts of Marcus Chance on Tuesday afternoon and evening. He says he was here."

"Well, he was."

"You were here too?"

"Well, I guess I was if I'm sayin' he was here."

"Did he stay the whole night?"

"Look. Why you come botherin' folks tryin' to sleep? I'm not feelin' good."

"I'm sorry, Mrs. James. But are you sure of that date?"

"Yes, I'm sure. Tuesday."

"And he was here all night?"

"Whole damn night."

"You could swear to that?"

"I certainly could."

He closed his notebook.

After he left, Cirri dashed across the room and hugged Mama. "Thank you!"

Mama pulled away and straightened the front of her dress. "I was wanting him out my house. Po-lice make me nervous." Then she went back to bed.

Cirri took Mama's defense of Marcus as a good sign. Mama must not mind if Cirri spent time with him. And Mama had stood there just fine, hadn't she? Talked right up to the policeman and made him leave. Maybe she wasn't as bad off as Cirri worried she was. Maybe she could do fine if Cirri went back to school.

She went back on Monday. She and Marcus walked to classes hand in hand. If they didn't have a class together, she waited outside the door after the bell rang. He came for her and walked her to her next class before going to his own.

She stayed inside at lunchtime and bought food with money he gave her while he went outside to conduct his business. She didn't bother him about it anymore. She didn't want to say anything that might make him think she was upset with him. He had given her a leather jacket lined with wool. "I don't want you to ever be cold," he'd said.

He always came for her as the bell for the end of lunch was about to ring and snacked on something from her tray. Then they strolled to class together. He was invariably in a good mood—strutting along, speaking to everyone, his arm slung up over her shoulder.

Each day Cirri cut her last class—math, which she hated anyway—so she could make it to Pea and Willie's bus stop in time. Then they went home and watched TV or played with the kitten. Mama was gone by then. Marcus came in at dinnertime like a regular husband and father. He brought groceries. Cirri fixed some supper. They did homework together, put the kids to bed and went to bed themselves.

Every day, simple as it was, felt like a holiday. Cirri couldn't sleep at night for loving Marcus. She put her arms around him as he slept and thought about how much things had changed in only a few days. Everything had gone from dead and impossible to a life filled with possibilities. She wasn't hungry anymore. Once in a while she still worried that he would find someone else to replace her, but she pushed the thought back down. She couldn't think that of him now because he was everything to her—her man, friend, father.

In Mrs. Mitchell's class, Cirri struggled to remember rules about how to correct run-on sentences and sentence fragments. They had five minutes to do ten sentences out of the book. Mrs. Mitchell walked slowly around the room, looking over their shoulders, commenting to kids here and there.

When she reached Cirri's desk, she stooped down and whispered, "I tried to call you last week."

"Why?"

"Wondered where you were. One of my best students. I missed your bright and beautiful face."

Mrs. Mitchell was forever saying something dumb like that, but Cirri liked it. "Got no phone," Cirri said.

"So I found out. Where had you been keeping yourself?"

Cirri glanced at Marcus, then down at the unfinished sentences on her paper. "I needed to take care of my Mama."

"Has she been sick?"

"Yeah."

"I told Marcus to bring you back to school. I'm glad he listens to me so well."

Cirri smiled, then covered her mouth.

"Is your mother better?"

"Getting better. I thought it was time to get back here."

Mrs. Mitchell patted Cirri's hand. "I'm glad you thought that. It's a good choice."

After they finished the sentences and corrected them, they spent some time talking about the Zora Neale Hurston book, *Their Eyes Were Watching God*. Marcus had told her what the first half of the book was about, and she'd read the last few chapters herself—about the hurricane and Janie realizing that Tea Cake really did love her, then Tea Cake's awful death.

After they discussed their feelings about Tea Cake and Janie, Mrs. Mitchell said, "Okay, now I want you to write a two-page essay with the title, 'How do I know when love is real?' With Tea Cake and Janie it was man-and-woman love, but I want you to consider all kinds of love—parents and children, brothers and sisters, *and* man-and-woman love, if you think you've got that all figured out."

Cirri peeked at Marcus. He grinned his big silly grin, which made her giggle, but she kept it to herself.

"No sentence fragments or run-ons," Mrs. Mitchell went on. "I want to see your ideas and quality thoughts. I also want to see grammatical perfection on paper."

After class, Marcus squeezed her shoulder and tickled her neck as they walked down the corridor. "You love me, Cirri James? Is your love real?" he asked.

The question hurt her because she loved him so much that she couldn't joke about it the way he did. "You're about as high-jivin' as Tea Cake," she snapped.

"Tea Cake loved that woman," Marcus reminded her.

"Not that she ever knew it."

"She knew it at the end."

"Uh huh, what use to her was he at the end? Sick ol' thing. She had to just go on and shoot him."

Marcus whirled her into a corner of the stairwell hidden from the corridor. He pinned her against the wall. "Someone gotta be a use to you before you love 'em?" He wasn't joking this time.

"No," she said simply.

"Why you talk like this, then?"

"I thought we were just jivin'."

"You wanna see me shot someday?"

She shook her head. This wasn't the Marcus she knew.

Something else was going on. She touched his face. "You in trouble, baby?"

That seemed to help. His smile returned. "Naw!" But the sincerity in his eyes lapsed for a second. She knew he was lying. "I gotta work tonight, baby," he said. "Let's go back to your house now."

"What you mean, work?"

He tilted his head. "Just something I gotta do." He pushed his hips into hers. "We could get close right now."

"Mama's home now," she said.

He kissed her nose, then her lips, held her tight against him. "*Do* you love me, Cirri?"

She whispered, "Yes."

He grinned. "Good."

He seemed to be needing her, wanting to hold on to her. "Tell me what's happening," she mumbled, their faces cheek-to-cheek.

"Ain't nothin' happening."

Then Mrs. Mitchell caught them. "Under the stairway. You two!" she shouted. "I thought you'd be a good match, but maybe I never should have encouraged it. This is no lover's lane. Let's go."

They broke apart, but still held hands. "We were testing out the assignment," Marcus said. "About 'Is love real?' "

"English is not a lab course," Mrs. Mitchell grumbled. "No experiments required."

On this first night in over a week that Marcus did not show up for supper, Cirri worried about him. She was short-tempered with Pea and Willie. Her mind darted from one thought to the next: Where was he? What was happening to him? Was there anything she could do? She regretted not coming home with him today during school as he had suggested. They could have been quiet enough not to wake Mama.

Now he wouldn't come back to her until nearly morning. She wished she'd thought earlier about how much she'd be missing him and given him what he'd wanted, so he could truly know, wherever he was tonight, that her love was real.

Pea and Willie were going to sleep on the couch. The TV was off. She sat at the kitchen table hunched over the blank piece of notebook paper that Mrs. Mitchell had given her.

She wrote, *How do I know when love is real?* on the title line.

The question brought up so many thoughts. She got up and walked to where she could see the kids. Furry was curled up by where their feet met on the couch. They were almost asleep. Pea had her thumb in her mouth. She waved at Cirri with her fingers, not letting up on her sucking. Then she closed her eyes. Willie stared at the ceiling. She went back to the table and wrote.

Love is a feeling you have in your hart that make you want to pertect and take care of people. It make you happy when their happy it make you scared and worryed if there in a dangrous situation it make you want to be around those people more than any other people and you miss them like theres a hole in your hart when their gone. It make you forgive things they've done if some times they've done wrong things.

I know this is love because I feel it for sevral people—for my brother and sister for my mother and father and for Marcus Chance. The hard part is knowing if they love you back as much as you love them in this I can understand Janies feelings about Tea Cake.

My brother and sister love me but thats jus a childish thing because they don't no any diffrent. I believe my mother loves me altho she is sick right now and consirned only about her own troubles. I used to think my father loved me actually I thought he loved us all my mother most of all. But he hirt his back on the job and the man wouldn't pay the insurance and my father couldn't get no more work and then I think he started drugs cause his back hirt him alot and he couldn't werk My mother started using them to so she could be with him because she loved him very much. We had a very nise family and a very nise house but then he left and we didn't see him for a long time once he came back and stayed a few days he toll us he loved us and he was going to be a regular father again but then he left out again and he aint come back. My mother sometimes say shes going out to find him but mostly she doesn't want to talk about him because it hirt her to much. I know I would forgive him if he came back. Because I still do love him and miss him even after all this but I'm not sure he loves us other wise how could he stand to be away from us so long and not worry about us because he should worry about us were not always doing so good.

I love Marcus to I think you know that. He is the first boy I ever really loved. I think other times it was puppy love. Marcus has never said he loves me but it don't matter words are easy to say feelings are hard to measure. I think I'm going to get hirt like Mama but I don't care now. I love him to much I think women feel love deeper and want love more then men.

Marcus and Cirri left school early the next day to meet Pea and Willie at their bus stop. Marcus had told her he wanted to take them someplace. So they walked the five blocks over to the next bus line and waited in the cold. The bus came soon, and it wasn't a long ride until they were in a neighborhood of redbrick row houses with porches and little mats of lawns.

They followed Marcus up the walk of one of those houses.

Without knocking, he walked right in the front door. "Mimi!" he shouted.

"I'm here," a woman answered, coming up to Marcus, taking his face in her hands and kissing him square on the lips.

She was short and thin and her gray hair wasn't much longer than a boy's. She wore large hoops in her ears and a smaller hoop through one nostril.

"This is Cirri," Marcus announced, showing her off. "And this is the other woman in my life, Cirri. Mimi. That was the name I gave her when I was little. Other folks round here call her Grandma."

She pinched Marcus's cheek. "I like Mimi better." Then she stooped down. "And who else is here?"

"This is Pea and Willie," Cirri said.

"Uh huh," Mimi said. "Well, I'm glad you all came over because I made some banana pudding a while ago, and I was just sitting her wondering who was gonna eat it because I hate bananas. They make me burp. You think you might be able to help me empty some of it out of my refridge?"

"Let's go," said Marcus, "Mimi makes the best banana pudding."

"Oh, I wasn't inviting you two big horses. I know you'd eat it all up. I'm only asking these two fine youngsters here," Mimi said.

Pea was taken in by it. "Okay," she said softly.

Willie was a little more skeptical until Mimi held out her hand. Then he allowed her to walk him and Pea down the hall to the kitchen.

Marcus led Cirri up the stairs. There were pictures on all the walls—serious young faces in white caps and gowns, in confirmation clothes, in Navy uniforms, in wedding dresses, pictures of Dr. King and Malcolm X and Jesse Jackson and Louis Farrakhan.

Marcus pulled her into a room at the top of the stairs and shut the door. He held her face, as Mimi had held his, and kissed her. He ran his hands down her breasts. "Um. Um." He took a deep breath as if to calm down, then he threw himself down on one of the three beds. "This is my room," he said.

She looked around, wanting to gather everything in and memorize it. More pictures were hung on faded green wallpaper. A closet was open and bulging clothes. There was a red, yellow, and black flag on one wall, a table cluttered with books, lamps, boxes, a model airplane, yellow throw rugs on the floor.

"Who else stays in here?" she asked.

"Sometimes my cousin. Sometimes my uncle. Sometimes just anybody. She likes to help people out."

"Where's your mother?"

"Gone. Florida."

"Where's your father?"

"Who?"

"Why didn't your mother take you to Florida?"

"I didn't want to go. I don't get along with her too much. It was an agreement that I would stay with Mimi."

"Mimi don't care us being up here like this and her taking care of the kids?"

"I've told her all about you. She was the one told me to bring you over here. She wanted to meet you. She's a busybody. She's happy to take care of the kids 'cause she knows we'll come down soon and she can get all kinds of information out of us. You watch." Marcus laughed.

Cirri wondered what would happen if Mimi didn't like her. Her opinion would obviously carry a heavy weight with Marcus. She turned away from him, to hide her worry. She bent close to one of the pictures. "Who are all these people?"

"Folks. I don't know 'em all myself. She collects 'em. Relatives, people who've stayed here at one time or another. Neighbors. She knows 'em all, though, and the stories to go with 'em."

"What is this? A rooming house?"

"No. Just a regular house and a silly ol' woman who loves to get all up into other people's business."

"Your grandpa here too?"

"No. He's dead. She's got a little Social Security coming in, and the rest of us make up the difference."

"What do you mean?"

"People who stay here. We all pitch in on the bills and the groceries. And I got to do my part. That's why I work."

She sat down on the bed next to him. "There *is* McDonald's, you know."

He laughed. "Uh huh. And what'd you do about your application up there?"

"I got three people to take care of. I can't be working all hours of the day and night."

He pulled her down onto his chest and kissed her. "I got people to take care of, too," he whispered. "There's you. And there's Mimi. See, she's raisin' me up, givin' me good things. She doesn't have much. But whatever she has she gives to people. I gotta do my share, take care of her, too."

His kissing and holding her here in his house, in his own room, made her weak. The more of himself and his life he showed her, the more she loved him, the more she felt desperate and too alone without him. Before him, she had been strong. She could handle any disappointment, deal with any crisis. Now she felt vulnerable and weak. He had told her he would have to work tonight, and she was already scared. Already she knew she would be snappy and irritated with Pea and Willie, that she wouldn't sleep much until he came back.

She would have to hold back tears of relief when she felt him slide into bed next to her.

"Them kids eating up that banana pudding. Don't know what sweetness they missing up here," he murmured drowsily. "Got that sweetness with 'em all the time. Don't know how lucky they are."

"Marcus," she said. "What do you do when you work at night?"

He seemed to be falling asleep. "Nothing much. Stand around."

"Waiting for something?"

"Somebody."

"Who?" she asked.

"Nick Tiebault."

She pushed up from him. "Nick Tiebault! The white guy at school?"

He ran his finger across her lip. "The white guy with all the connections. But, you don't know a thing. You hear?"

"What do you do with him?"

"Pickup-and-delivery business. That's all. Simple as that."

"You're talking big time, now. Picking up loads and taking them somewhere else."

Marcus laughed and closed his eyes, tucked his hands under his head. "You don't even know the *meaning* of big time, dahlin'."

She was scared now. "I don't want you to do this anymore, Marcus."

Marcus opened his eyes and stared at the ceiling, sounding serious for once. "I've thought it all through. I don't want heavy shit no more than anyone else. But this isn't heavy. Everyone is careful. Everyone plays right with each other. And everyone profits." His eyes turned to her. "Fine profits, sweetheart. Can't argue with that."

She sat up straight. "Don't bring me no more groceries if I'm the cause of this. I got my groceries just fine before. I can do it again."

He chuckled. "I'm not talking about grocery money. I'm saving up. Gonna get a car. Gonna get together a down payment for a house maybe."

"You crazy!"

"You want to live with me in my house after I get it?"

She shot him a look, then stood up and walked across to the window, pushed aside the curtain, and looked at the sidewalk. Everything outside looked bleak and dead: dirty gray street and sidewalk, dried–up plants, dull, heavy sky. It was cold, too, although she was comfortable in here. She knew she would feel as cold and lifeless as the scene outside if anything every happened to Marcus. Neither of them spoke or moved for a long time.

Then, she heard the bed frame creak as he got up off it and came to her. "I always got to be coming to you, don't I, Cirri James?" He folded his arms around her. "That's okay, though. I like it. You an independent woman, like Mimi. You no sweet-assed fool who falls for any sweet-talking jive that comes along. You think things through."

She felt more scared and weak now than she had ever felt before. Here he was saying she was independent, and all she wanted was to slide in under his shirt and stay there.

When they came downstairs and walked into the kitchen, Mimi was talking to a tall, heavyset man who leaned against the counter and sipped from a mug. "I tole her a week ago to take that arm to the doctor. 'Could be a sprain,' I said, 'could be a break. What you gonna do? Keep driving that bus an' ack like you ain't hurtin'? What you gonna do if it is broke? No-body wants a broken-arm bus driver. They gonna put you on a desk job for six weeks. No big deal!' But did she listen to me?"

"What's happening now?" Marcus asked.

"It was broke and now it's growing back crooked. They gonna have to rebreak the bone," the man said.

"Lawd have mercy," Mimi said. "Don't even say it up in front of these children. Gives me the shivers to think about it. 'Course she didn't listen to me. Tell her, 'Don't ever listen to Mimi Chance.' "

Marcus got up but wouldn't let go of Cirri, so she had to get up too. He opened the refrigerator, handed Cirri a bowl of pudding, and took a spoon from the drain board.

"Lookit here these two Siamese twins joined at the hand, poor things," Mimi said.

Marcus grinned, and Cirri giggled, enjoying the silliness.

"Mimi said you couldn't have any pudding," Willie piped up.

Marcus pointed at the empty bowls on the table. "I see you enjoyed two bowlfuls, smart-face. Who's the horse, huh?"

"Lordie, Lordie," Mimi said, leaning over the sink to peer out the window. "Mr. Hatfield done put another dent in that car."

"How can you tell?" Marcus asked. "They so many already."

"I wish he wouldn't drive so fast. I tole him I don't want to be going to no funerals," Mimi clucked. She ran water in the sink and went on. "Marguerite's got her gran'babies over there today. I know she having a good day. Don't have to worry about her today. No siree. Those babies make her shine just fine."

"Jewel come back?" Marcus asked.

Mimi slapped the suds. "No. And I finished that hemming she needed."

Cirri sat enjoying the brightness in the kitchen, the pink plastic tablecloth, the smell of coffee brewing, and the easy talk and love in the room. Her home had felt like this once, a few years ago.

"You gonna be out tonight?" Mimi asked Marcus.

"Over at Cirri's," he said and winked at Cirri.

So Mimi didn't know about Marcus's night work, and Cirri was his alibi. She wondered whether Mimi knew about Marcus's work at all. Where did she think the money came from?

For a moment Cirri resented the fact that Mimi didn't know about Marcus's work. Cirri had to bear the worry alone. But, then, she was pleased. It was as it should be—she and Marcus were in this together. He had trusted her with the truth.

Marcus ate the last bite of the pudding himself, then kissed Cirri. " 'Bout time we go," he said and released her hand. "You kids ready?"

Cirri took her bowl and a couple of glasses to the sink. "I can wash these up, Mrs. Chance."

"Shoot fire. I know you *can*, but my hands are already wet."

"Where are their coats, Mimi?" Marcus asked.

"On the living-room couch."

He herded the kids that way.

"I do my best thinking and spying," Mimi said, studying the houses outside, "when my hands are wet. I love to wash dishes."

"The pudding was good."

She didn't seem to hear. "Marcus is a fine young man, ain't he?" she said, drying her hands on her apron.

"Yes, ma'am."

"He got in a little trouble a couple of weeks back. I had to go in to Dr. Jasper and get Marcus reinstated in school. Dr.

Jasper's a fine man. I've had, oh, 'round 'bout twelve or thirteen kids in that school one time or another. He said we could turn Marcus around, get him out of that mess, and I said, 'Yes sir, I knew we could.' Because Marcus is fine. Always has been. He's a favorite of mine. He is a sweet child." She had said all this looking out the window, as if talking to herself. Then she turned to Cirri. "But I think the best thing for him has been you. He's talkin' Cirri-this and Cirri-that. Going to Cirri's every night. I just had to meet you. And them kids are real cute." She paused and her face curved into a plea. "He's not back in that mess, is he?"

Cirri knew how Mimi felt. The aching worry was etched in the lines around her eyes. But Cirri also had a pact with Marcus. They were bound to each other like the stupid Siamese twins Mimi'd talked about.

"No, he's not in any mess," Cirri said, hoping she was telling the truth.

"Promise me you'll keep him out of it, won't you?"

"I will."

Then Mimi hugged Cirri, squeezed her and patted her back. "Good," she murmured. "Good."

Marcus sidled up next to her in bed sometime in the middle of the night. He was cold and he smelled like smoke. Cirri put her arms around him, glad he was back. But the smell bothered her. "Why you smell like this?"

"We watched a house burning. It was so cold the water the firemen were spraying froze."

"Whose house?"

"How'm I supposed to know?" He wiggled his hands up under her nightgown. "Get me warm, baby."

"Our friend Furry's house got burned 'cause he didn't pay off some hustlers."

He cupped his cold hands over her breasts. "I didn't have nothing to do with this fire."

He had on a T-shirt but no underwear. He pushed his hips against her, mashed his hard thing against her thigh. She hugged him tighter, ran her hands down to the round cheeks of his backside.

He shivered. "Warm me up, baby."

He rolled up on top of her and she spread her legs. He kissed her with his tongue in her mouth and pushed himself inside her. As he kept kissing her and pushing himself in and out, she thrust up her chest because she liked to feel her breasts pressed against him. He groaned two or three times, then did a kind of dance, and with one last, hard push he buried his face in her shoulder and collapsed on top of her. In the sudden calm, she could feel it jerking inside.

She ran her hand over his head like she was petting a puppy. This was the part that she always liked most of all. They were linked, he was relaxed and tender, gently stroking her lip with one finger. He was a solid, warm, blanket of weight upon her.

Only, she wished his hair didn't smell of smoke, because she'd made that promise to Mimi.

Heck

IN THE MONTHLY FACULTY
meetings, Heck let other members of the staff make their reports first while he sat and listened. He heard security report that there had been sixteen fights, eight assaults and three arrests in and around the school in the last month. Of the arrests, two had been Grant students selling crack. The third had been a vagrant exposing himself to students. The assaults had mostly been one kid beating up on another one, but two of them had involved weapons—a knife and a brick.

In the last few years, such incidents had been on the rise. Sure, high tempers and emotions were part of the territory with teenagers. But now every other day there was some new explosive event at school, and he didn't know how to handle it anymore. Security usually took over. They controlled the school.

Grant wasn't the only school where this had happened. All

of the schools had security details. They wore yellow jackets and carried walkie-talkies so they could be in constant contact with other members of the detail while they patrolled the halls. And principals had responded in various ways. Some principals had become basically another member of security. They roamed the halls murmuring into their own walkie-talkies about smoking in a lavatory, about loiterers outside the cafeteria, about trouble brewing in a classroom, about illegal-looking paraphernalia in a stairway. Some, not wanting to disrupt students with the constant chatter on the walkie-talkie, wore an ear wire, so that only they heard the reports. Plugged in this way, they listened more to security than to anyone else.

Heck believed he wasn't paid to be a policeman. He didn't think a school should be a place of control and coercion and apprehension. He wanted it to be a place of revelation and opportunity. So his walkie-talkie stayed on his assistant principal's desk, while he tried other ways to curb the disorders.

He brought in police for assemblies about teenage crime and detention-center conditions. He tried to keep track of offenders if they didn't come back to school. He promoted school-spirit days during which teachers were supposed to address the problems as a blight on the school. Students were told that they should conduct themselves with maturity in order to be as proud of themselves as they were of the football team. He initiated in-school community-service suspensions for offenders. Rather than throw them out of school for three days, where they might get into more trouble, he put them to work scrubbing tile in the bathrooms, changing light bulbs, painting over graffiti. And while he supervised their work, he tried to get them to talk about themselves, so he could find a way to reach them.

But the statistics rose. With many kids he never found an

opening. He just disciplined them harshly and set them adrift. With the others, he still tried, but he wasn't often hopeful.

"And then there was the incident in Dr. Jasper's office," the security officer went on. "The police are in on this one, of course. But if any of you overhear any kind of talk, please let us know."

"Are we assuming it was a student, then?" someone asked.

"We don't know. It would be nice if security here could come up with some kind of lead." He put a hand on one hip just above where the walkie-talkie hooked onto his belt. "It'd be a real nice feather in our caps."

The man, still with his hand on his hip, comfortable at the podium, was answering questions. And the teachers were attentive. Times had changed.

"Dr. Canaletti wants test scores," Heck said when it was his turn. He was weary. "New, improved, first-rate test scores. Now, I think you know how I feel about this . . ."

"We know how you feel about *him*," someone said, and got a laugh.

Heck ignored this. ". . . but we really should try to give the man something. So I've drawn up a few suggestions here." He handed a stack of papers to a man in the front row to be passed out. "These are ways to maximize teaching time in your fifty minutes. Nothing new. Just a few reminders and time-proven tricks. I expect you to use these. Sharpen up your act. Focus. Use every minute. Maybe that way, you can squeeze in some test preparation as a complement to whatever else you're doing.

"More important than this, however, is that I want you to be on the phone. This is mid-November. Who is not in your class now who was there in September? What happened to them? Call and remind them about that good paper they handed in. Tell them you enjoyed their intelligent comments during the class discussions. *Encourage* them to come back to school."

There was a hum in the room. Several teachers near the back were talking. Shunks was at the hub.

"We owe it to these kids. We're the only ones saying to them that school is where they should be, not because of the law, but because of them. They deserve it." Then he bellowed. "Shunks, if you can't shut your mouth, then leave the room!"

He took a deep breath. "And those kids who are here one or two days a week. Tell them what they're good at. Find out why the assignments aren't coming in. It's okay to get into their business. You might be the only adult talking to that child in any reasonable way. *Care* about them. It *might* keep 'em coming." He stopped and squeezed the bridge of his nose. He was repeating himself. "You've heard this before," he said. "This is *my* agenda."

"Maybe it was Canaletti that trashed your office," Shunks called out.

Everyone laughed. Heck ignored him. "Meeting adjourned," he said, feeling hopeless.

Maintenance had removed the cabinet door frames from his office since it would be too much work and money to replace all the glass. They had puttied the screw holes, sanded and painted the shelves a warm brown that looked almost like walnut. Then, as a favor to Heck, they had painted the rest of the wood trim in the room—the window frames, the baseboards, the doors—the same walnut shade and replaced the glaring yellow that Heck hated with a soft beige.

Heck still had to reshelve all the books which were stacked on the floor. He also needed to reorganize and reclaim his desk. He had been using one in the outer office while the painting was going on. His own desk was covered with dusty mail, half-finished paperwork, scattered notes to himself, broken odds and ends that had been salvaged from the wreckage. There was one more week before Thanksgiving break. He had set himself the goal of having everything straightened out by then, including finding the culprit. He had formulated a short list of suspects, and he frequently reviewed it, thinking about each name. He had figured out access to the keys for most of them. The police had called. They wanted to meet with him. He thought they were probably closing in.

He blew the dust off some papers on his desk and tried to remember where he'd left off. But he soon heard a row in the outer office and stepped out to see what was happening. Mr. and Mrs. Cooper were arguing with Ann, the secretary. They were side by side, holding hands, both talking at the same time.

"What's the problem?" he asked.

"We would like to talk to you," Mr. Cooper said. "You didn't answer our letter."

"I told them they need to call and schedule a time," Ann said.

"Yes, that's true," Heck answered, to help Ann out, "but since they're here now and I have a minute, it'll be all right. Why don't you folks come on in?"

"I'm sorry I don't have any chairs in here," Heck said, ushering them into his office. "The place is being painted."

"I know what happened," Mrs. Cooper snarled, pointing a finger. She had a Band-Aid across the bridge of her nose. "Someone busted up the place. Anya told me. Lotta things not right at this school."

Mr. Cooper tightened his arm around his wife's waist and shook her a little to calm her down. The black thread of stitches stuck out on his ear. "We come about our letter about that teacher, Miz Brown. She's preaching racism. And we think she oughta be fired. Why didn't you answer our letter?"

The letter had come last Friday, two days after the office had been broken up. It was an ungrammatical, incoherent piece of work full of veiled threats to Miz Brown and to himself. He knew the Coopers were strange. He was feeling disorganized and attacked from all sides at the time, so he had put it aside.

"She's saying whites are responsible for all the troubles of the blacks. Now come on! She's got those kids in there believing it. And the black kids are wanting to beat up the white kids. Now lookit little Anya . . ."

"That lady's promoting race warfare," Mr. Cooper said. "What does this have to do with education?"

"Anya comes home scared," Mrs. Cooper said. "Can't sleep. She tells me these things. We're this close. Twin sisters couldn't be closer'n my daughter an' me."

"This is public education at its worst," Mr. Cooper interrupted. "We're going to take this up with our elected officials if we don't get some satisfaction from you."

Mrs. Cooper smiled at her husband's eloquence and kissed him.

"So, are you gonna fire her?"

Heck spread his hands. "I can't fire her even if I wanted to. Tenured teachers are next to impossible to dislodge."

"Well, that's a hell of a thing," Mr. Cooper said. "If I'm not doing *my* job I get fired."

Mrs. Cooper looked Heck up and down. "Maybe Dr. Jasper thinks the woman *is* doing her job."

"Do you?"

"It's not your usual teaching style. She's very passionate . . ."

"There, you see."

". . . and she speaks to a good many students."

"Black students! That's the problem of sending a child to a school where she's in the minority."

"She has to hear all this hateful stuff."

"And you agree with the teacher, Dr. Jasper. I can tell you do. You believe in the same 'passions.' " Mrs. Cooper twisted the word.

"Anya is among the minority in this school," Heck said, raising his voice. "But she gets as good an education as any child in this school. And if she hears something about black history and black pride and black people taking control of their lives along the way, so much the better. She'll be a better-rounded individual for it."

"This ain't black history she's telling us about. The girl is scared, I tell you," Mrs. Cooper shrieked.

Heck wanted to wind this up. "All right. Let me go and sit in on Miz Brown's class. I'll speak to Anya. Then I'll get back to you."

Mrs. Cooper curled her lip. "You're not gonna do anything. I bet you don't do a thing. This school sucks. I'm gonna transfer my baby out. Get her away from all these attitudes and violence. Lookit this office."

She headed for the door and Mr. Cooper followed, grabbed her hand. "We'll be hearing from you, then?" he asked.

"If you want to."

Miz Brown had been teaching basically the same things since she'd come to Grant. Heck supposed she had taught that way in New York, too, where she and her husband had lived before he had been transferred to Washington. "These kids are complacent," she often said. "They don't know there are still battles to be fought in this country. They don't have any idea that they are the ones who have to rise up and scream about lousy health services and housing and unemployment."

She taught a little history, too. But, basically, the kids got a yearlong tirade about America's inherent racism and their need to do something about it. While it wasn't brilliant teaching and it certainly did not help them when it came to American history questions on the standardized tests, Heck didn't think it was all bad, either. The kids needed to hear that they had to fight for what they wanted. They needed to hear that racism still existed in this country despite Dr. King and all kinds of civil-rights legislation. Maybe she was a little hysterical, but at least she had the kids' best interests at heart.

He wished sometimes that the intercoms in the classrooms didn't produce so much static so he could listen in. His presence in a room usually changed what went on there. Miz Brown, however, loved to have him come into her room, as if he were another paying customer coming to see her act. Just as she included kids in her act, day after day, she drew him in also, used him as part of the lesson.

He nodded to her as he closed the door and took a seat in the back. She was waving a folded newspaper, then slapping it against her thigh.

Figures were written on the blackboard:

Lack of early prenatal care	DC 50th
Infant mortality	DC 51st
% of children in poverty	DC 49th
% not finishing school	DC 51st
Juvenile incarceration	DC 51st

She paced in front of the board, slapping her thigh, "Are we talking about old people here?"

The class murmured, "No."

"Are we talking about rich people here?"

"No."

"Are we talking about white people here?"

"No."

"What is the racial makeup of this town we're living in?"

"Seventy-five percent black."

"Are you old, rich, white or stupid?"

"No."

She stopped and raised the newspaper. "Then who are they talking about in these statistics?"

"Us."

"And what are you going to do about it? What can you do about it? You're letting these people keep you down. And this is your own life. Your one and only life. You going to live *all* your life at the bottom of the pile? Fifty-first. There are only fifty states in this country. We're *below* fifty. That's how bad it is. Akeesha. Stand up."

Akeesha Melvin stood up.

"Didn't you tell me last week," Miz Brown asked, "that you were thinking about quitting school and getting a job?"

"Yeah."

"Have you got that job?"

"Not yet."

"It was going to be vacuuming the fitting rooms in a department store, wasn't it?"

"Yes."

"And getting down on your hands and knees to pick the pins out of the carpet that the ladies carelessly drop when they are trying on garments?"

Akeesha raised one shoulder. "I guess."

"And scraping off the slimy gum full of who-knows-what-germs that the teenagers drop on the carpet?"

Akeesha giggled and put a hand to her mouth.

"And maybe, if you're lucky, putting all the clothes back on the hangers, making them look nice again, and taking them back out onto the sales floor."

"Sure."

"All those clothes you won't hardly ever be able to buy yourself because your pay is so low. You'll be able to see those clothes and make those fine clothes look nice again on the hangers. But they're never gonna hang on you if you don't finish school. Is it worth it? That great job you'll have? To be bottom, below all the other people in all the other states for the rest of your life? Fifty-first?"

"I don't guess so."

"Sit down, Akeesha. Thank you. Think about it, please."

"White people want you to take those dead-end, 'ain't goin' nowhere' jobs. You're playing right into their hands. They want to hang on to their notions that black folks are dumb—can't even finish school. They're lazy. They take the simplest, low-down, dirtiest jobs because they don't want to work hard for anything better. They got no ambition or desire to better themselves. They are willing to stay fifty-first. Lord have mercy!"

Heck watched the two white children in the class—Anya and Nick Tiebault. Anya wasn't squirming or showing any other particular signs of distress. Tiebault was staring out the window, chin raised, looking madder than hell. If either child were being affected here, Heck worried more about Tiebault.

Miz Brown dropped the newspaper on her desk. She paused for effect and strolled over to the window as if she were suddenly interested in the weather. The class watched her in silence. "Now there's something else, too," she said. "We've talked about it before. There's murder and death and pain and agony for black people of all ages out there on the street. And it comes from the latest oppressor. You know what I'm talking about."

"Drugs," a few murmured.

"That's right," she said quietly. "So you're going to try it, just a few times. Go ahead. That's just what they want you to do. The white folks, the politicians, the powers that be."

She turned to him. "Dr. Jasper, could you tell me something?"

"Yes, ma'am."

"Do you think students who are high on something or other can pay attention well in class?"

"I doubt it."

"Would they be responsible enough to do their assignments and get them in on time?"

"Probably not."

"So, if they don't pay attention in class or even come to class, and they don't do their assignments, how do they pass their tests?"

He played along. "They probably don't pass their tests."

"Which means they don't pass the subject or be promoted or ever graduate. So, there we are. Fifty-first again."

"That's right."

"Right where the white folks want us. Not causing any trouble to them, not challenging them or their self-proclaimed superiority. We help them sleep at night, cozy in the knowledge that their stereotypes and racist ideas are not disturbed.

"Meanwhile, what are we doing?" She raised her voice to a shout. "We're down here shooting each other in the head and selling each other the dope and starving our babies to pay the white man for the stuff. Because he's the one selling it to us. And he's the one not doing anything to stop it infecting everybody's lives, he's the one lynching us, once again. Only this time he's getting rich while he's watching us lynch each other.

'Cause I'll tell you something—dead is dead whether it's from hanging from a tree branch or it's from a bullet in the brain!"

The students chanted a response and pounded a rhythm on their desks at the same time. "And it's my life, to live and to own."

"There's only one life."

"And it's my life, to live and to own."

"Dr. Jasper, have you ever seen students in this very school on something or carrying something related to drug trafficking?"

"Yes, ma'am, I have."

"And what happens to those students?"

"First, they are suspended. Their parents have to come in. We try to find them some help. The next time, they are expelled. If I see them around the school after that, I call the police."

"Have you expelled many students?"

"Quite a few."

"Called the police on many?"

"Three or four."

"Have many Grant students gone to jail?"

"Over the years, too many."

"Jail is also a good place for black folks to be, especially the men. The white people say, 'We always have felt better about those darkies when we could have them under lock and key.' "

After the bell rang, he stood in the corridor, as he frequently did, to assure an orderly change of classes and to be available to students.

Marcus Chance passed by. "I'm going to your teen nights," he said. "Whooping their tails off with a paddle and a little ball."

"Keep it up, son, I'm getting my reports from Van."

Anya Cooper hurried past him toward her next class. "Miss Cooper," he shouted after her.

"Yes."

"Come here, dear." She held her books in front of her chest defensively. Her shoulders were stooped. "I'll give you a late pass. But come now and walk this way with me for a minute."

She didn't say a word, but fell into step with his slow gait. "Tell me, how is school going for you this year?"

"All right."

"Got some friends?"

"A couple."

"Like your teachers?"

"I like Mrs. Mitchell. I wish I had her again this year. She's nice."

"Yes, she is. And your other teachers?"

"They're okay. Nothing special."

"Miz Brown, for instance. We just came from her class."

"I don't think she cares about the white kids, but there aren't too many of us anyway."

"But she should be caring about all of her students, shouldn't she?"

"Yeah, but that's pretty hard to do, I know."

"Do any of the things she says frighten you? I mean she wasn't being too kind about white folks in there today."

"Oh, today was better than some days. But I don't think anybody's going to kill me, if that's what you mean. I'm not holding anyone down myself, you know. I've got it rougher'n a lot of kids in this school. Mrs. Mitchell knows all about it."

"All right. I'll assume, then, that if anything is bothering you, you'll take it to Mrs. Mitchell or to myself. Anything at all. Okay?"

When the girl smiled, she revealed green teeth that hadn't been brushed. "Okay."

"Do I have your word?"

"Yes."

He sent Anya to class and walked slowly back to the office. So she was using Miz Brown to pull her parents together. If they were fighting someone outside the family, then they didn't have to fight each other. It was a good tactic, one that was working for her, at least for now. Of course, he was the one caught in the bind—what to tell the Coopers; not to reveal Anya's strategy. Maybe a lot of what she was doing was unconscious anyway. Yet he needed to reassure the parents that all was under control at school. Because they could cause some awkward scenes, all of which would be painful for Anya.

He went over his mental list again. The most likely suspect was Guy Tomblin, even though he wasn't a student. He was experienced with metal. Keys could be made from wax imprints. He had access to the shop teacher's keys. He wanted to get back at Heck for having him watched. Scrupulous behavior was not part of his makeup.

Then there was George Hammond, the kid he'd sent to prison last year. George had stabbed another student for owing him money. It was about time for him to be paroled. Only problem was, How did he get into the school and into the office?

Marcus Chance. Heck didn't really think Marcus would have done it. Marcus was an enigmatic kid. He was popular with students and teachers. Heck himself felt the power of Marcus's personality. He was confident and at ease, handsome and unusually friendly. Teachers would give him keys and send him to the storeroom for books or paper, to their cars for things they'd forgotten There was another side to him, too. He was a hustler. Heck knew that, but because he wasn't a big-time hustler, wasn't in so deep yet, Heck was trying to ignore this while he worked with him.

Heck hoped the police had some answers. He wanted this embarrassment, this sign of weakness, behind him.

He had chairs brought into his office so the officers could sit down, but Officer Robinson stood like a student reading a report. He probably felt like a student again, here, in front of Heck. Robinson had graduated from Grant several years earlier. They had talked about that when he had first come to investigate. Heck had remembered him and congratulated him on his fine job, the success he had made of himself.

"We have the results of the lab work, sir," Robinson said somberly. "Most all of the fingerprints we found were yours, as would be expected. There were some others, but we have no files on them."

"Fifty people a day come and go in here," Heck said. "You know that. Parents, teachers, students, my secretary . . . fin-gerprints, I don't know." Heck shook his head. "It seems so inexact." He went on, thinking aloud. "But then you'd have Tomblin's on file, wouldn't you? And his didn't show up?"

"That doesn't necessarily mean anything, though. The most remarkable result, though, was something we'd suspected. The stuff on your desk, sir."

"Yes?"

"It was semen."

Outraged, Heck shouted, "You mean to tell me someone jacked off onto my desk?"

"Not exactly, sir. It seems there was also a female."

"What?"

"We had it all tested. There was a used condom in the trash basket."

"Jesus Christ! So, someone fucked on my desk."

Robinson was quiet while Heck circled his desk.

"That means we're looking for two people, not just one," Robinson put in.

"My God," Heck said. "What if Tomblin got one of the girls in here . . ."

"Tomblin, sir, has a pretty good alibi. We're going to have to be thinking of someone else. He was with a girlfriend that evening and all night. Stayed at her place. She swears to it. So does her roommate. That'd probably hold up in court."

"So who else?"

Robinson referred to his notes. "Marcus Chance says he was with Cirrus James that night. Know her?"

"But if they'd do it, they'd lie about it together, wouldn't they? Where did they stay? Where were their parents?"

"They were at Cirrus James's house. Her mother swears to it."

"The mother let them spend the night together? You believe that?"

"She swears he was there."

Heck sat down. His legs were aching. "Who else is there?"

"George Hammond, the kid you testified against last year, was paroled in October. But he was in the hospital on that night with a couple of broken ribs. We have the hospital records."

"Jesus! I thought you were going to come in here with answers today, get this thing over with!"

"We're focusing on Theodore Fuller, known as T-man," Robinson said steadfastly. "Trying to track him down."

"Why him?"

"You told us you'd suspended him two days before the incident and that he'd been pretty worked up about it at the time. His uncle, a Mr. Lamont Fuller, was recently on trial for stealing from school buildings. He's with city building maintenance. They have full sets of keys for emergency situations."

Heck rubbed his eyes with one hand. He had trouble focusing on all of this. There was a certain logic to it that he was aware of. But all he could understand was that he seemed to have a lot of enemies and somehow they were all more clever and quick-witted than he was.

"Mr. Fuller was acquitted, but T-man could have gotten hold of the keys, you see."

"Acquitted on a technicality," Heck mumbled.

"That's right, sir. We're going to keep trying to find him, but we've had no luck so far. He might have hightailed it out of town for a while."

Heck nodded, doubtful that they would ever know who had done it.

"And my captain says this isn't high priority. There's no homicide involved, for instance. Just vandalism. I can't spend much more time on it, sir."

Heck felt sorry for Robinson then. He put his arm around the young officer's shoulders. He heaved in a breath. "I appreciate your efforts, son. I certainly do."

Maybe underneath it all, he thought as he walked toward Danny's office, one of the reasons he got rid of Tomblin was so he could have Danny back in the afternoons. When she carpooled with Tomblin, she left at a regular time every day, and she wasn't available to chat. He had missed their talks.

"Dr. Jasper," she said as he limped in. Her voice gave him the feeling she had missed him, too.

"You're not going to believe this, Danny," he said collapsing into a chair.

"What?"

"The police think T-man did my office, but they can't find him. The really big news, though, is that he used my desk to fuck on."

"How do they know that?"

"Condom in the trash. Semen on the desk."

"At least it was safe sex."

"Thanks."

"Coffee?"

"Yeah, give me some."

She fixed two cups, handed him his.

"I liked it better not knowing who it was," he said. "I don't want it to be T-man. I halfway liked the kid. I wanted it to be someone I hated."

"Skunks?"

Heck thought about it. "Yeah. See, he has a motive. I'm on his back. He has the keys."

"The stuff on the desk doesn't fit, though."

"Why not?"

"What woman would have him? Biggest thing about him is his mouth."

"Jesus, Danny!" Heck exclaimed, then broke out laughing. "You know who else I would've liked it to be?"

"Who?"

"The Coopers. You know Anya Cooper's parents?"

"Aw, Jeez. Now you're getting far-fetched."

"No, they're a regular Romeo and Juliet, demented-style. And they hate my guts."

"Yeah?"

"They were in my office yesterday. Managed some pretty heavy foreplay right in front of me."

"Was that before or after they knocked each other around?"

"Looked like after, judging from the stitches and Band-Aids."

"Great family environment there." She gulped some coffee. "I've never been especially turned on by that office. But all of a sudden you're making it sound like a tantalizing spot."

The coffee was terrible, but the conversation was good, as always. He stretched out his legs and crossed his ankles. Maybe this was what he needed, to be able to laugh for a while. He'd gotten himself all wound up.

He and Danny shared the same philosophy about kids and schools. Even though she was white, he felt comfortable with her, more comfortable than with any other whites he knew. He had learned he could trust her to be open and honest and not have any patronizing or judgmental agendas lurking behind her words. At one time he'd worried that he was falling into the oldest of the stereotypic traps—the black man craving the white woman and rejecting his own. But once he looked at it reasonably, he realized that all he really craved was her humor.

"I wanted it to be Miz Brown," Danny said. "Then maybe you'd finally get rid of her."

"Careful. Don't let your prejudices show."

"Yeah, I'm prejudiced against bad teaching and psychos."

"Consciousness-raising. That's what she does. It's important."

"You're nuts."

"Well, it wasn't Tomblin," Heck said. "I thought it was him for sure."

"Our Man of Perpetual Obscenity," she said casually.

Heck nodded. "He had a good alibi."

"What?"

"A woman."

"A woman!"

"You say that like you're jealous."

She put down her cup. "That fucker! Yes, I am."

Now he was mad. "What are you telling me? After three years of celibacy, whining about how you can't find a good man, you're making it with a convict?"

"He's an *ex*-convict."

"So?"

"There has been no 'making' anything."

"I hope not. You deserve something better."

"I'll be the judge of that. Okay, Dad?"

"I'm looking out for your best interests."

"Spare me."

"How's Rolls?"

"Fine," she said without thinking, then she added, "He needs a man around."

"Not that kind of man."

"Hey, why didn't you tell me Guy's status here in the first place? Strange kind of program, isn't it?"

"Recycles people. Gives 'em a break. The kids are supposed to learn from the convict's mistakes. We weren't supposed to tell anyone about his past so there would be no prejudice. I thought it was worth a try. I just didn't think we'd get a white guy."

"You weren't prejudiced about *him*?"

"Doesn't it make sense, with our population, that we get a black man?"

"To be a role model?"

"Well, it was a crackpot program, I guess. And then we get this foul-mouthed loser."

"He *did* care about the kids."

"The female ones."

"Shop boys loved him."

"He's gone. One less headache."

"How's your headache named Tina these days?"

"An obnoxious teenager. How is she in class? You working on speeches?"

"Debates. Two kids working together on opposite sides of issues."

"They do research at the library for this?"

"I hope so."

Heck felt better. "Well, maybe she's finally going to take it seriously. Seems like she's been doing some work for your class."

"Good. What's with the earrings?"

He feigned surprise. "I'm shocked at you. Don't you know an African-American fashion statement when it stares you in the face? One that says that a child is not going to be anything like her parents?"

"My gosh, you're right. Now that you mention it, that *was* what was written on that sign she was carrying. 'My parents suck eggs!' "

Heck laughed, feeling much better.

Danny

WHEN GUY CALLED TO ASK
Danny to go with him to Maryland's Eastern Shore on Saturday, she was not inclined to talk to him. She wanted to know
about the other woman and why he had never mentioned her.
At the same time, she knew she had no claim on him. Actually,
she should be grateful; he wanted to include Rolls. The day
out would do them good. So she agreed, but she didn't act en-
thusiastic because she was still peeved.

Guy picked them up in the truck, and they started for the
Bay Bridge. The morning was chilly, but the sun was warm.
Guy predicted that they would shed their coats by afternoon
for the picnic.

He had a disconcerting way of springing surprises on her
that she didn't like. "What picnic?" she asked.

He jerked his head toward the back of the truck. "I brought

some Italian subs. Made 'em myself. It's a specialty of mine. You like subs, Rolls?"

"Sure."

Danny was glad to hear the enthusiasm in Rolls's voice, but she still wished Guy would let her in on these things: that he'd done time, that he was seeing another woman, that he'd planned out the whole day including picnic and probably the weather.

"I brought a blanket," Guy said. "I know a nice spot where we can watch the Canadian geese."

She crossed her arms and settled in, satisfied for now. "Okay."

There wasn't much traffic. Every mile they drove farther from school and home in the sunshine lifted her spirits. She squeezed Rolls's knee playfully, as she often did, and he smiled.

"So, how's the ol' school?" Guy asked.

"Don't bring it up," Danny said.

"Jeez. Things that bad?"

"I guess they're no worse than normal."

"Find the office-smasher?"

"They think they know who it is. Haven't caught him yet, though."

"Cops came sniffing around me again."

"I heard."

"I told 'em to back off. I already lost that job, even though I wasn't guilty. And if they kept bugging me, they were going to make it look bad for me on my new one."

She couldn't resist. "Your alibi vouched for you."

"She told me all about it." He coughed. "She's trying to keep in my good graces, but she's driving me nuts. Thinks she owns me. Jeez, we been divorced for two and a half years. And she divorced me!"

"Divorced? I didn't know you were married!"

"When I got sent up, she divorced me. Now I'm out, she wants me back."

"Were you with her that night?"

"Sure. I been staying there, with her and her roommate. Two-bedroom place. It's bigger than mine."

Danny rolled her eyes and wondered how he could be so naive about the effects his actions had on people. "You mystify me."

"Why?"

"Why do you stay if you don't want to encourage her? Besides, I thought you had this special apartment just for people in the program."

"Aw, that place stinks. Staying with her is more comfortable. We're used to each other. She hates you, though. Whooee!"

"I can see why! How can you be so dense when it comes to women, and girls, and what you say to them, how you make them feel?"

"Cheryl doesn't care. She knows what's going on. I've told her. I'm just weaning her off."

"How kind of you."

"What do you mean? I'm the one being used. She dropped me flat after the conviction. Couldn't wait to be rid of me. Think that didn't hurt? Then she realized she'd had it pretty good with me after all and wanted me back. Soft-hearted dope that I am, I went over there when she called. It relieved my loneliness, I'll admit. But now, I'm thinking twice."

Rolls was hearing it all. Danny knew he wouldn't approve. And she felt a fool herself. "Well, maybe we shouldn't do this."

"Do what? On my day off I'd like to get out of town, see

some water, have a picnic. Cheryl doesn't have any claim on me. Besides, she's working. You're off."

"There you go again."

"What?"

"Sticking your foot in your mouth. Cheryl's working. My hours are more convenient."

"You want me to take you out somewhere on a school day? I want to go with you. Give me a break."

They were quiet then as the truck hummed along. She felt less annoyed than she was pretending to be. She kind of enjoyed bugging Guy. His backpedaling was funny to listen to. It felt good to hear him say, "I want to go with you."

The light, the cattails and the fields were all golden when they got out of the truck beside a small deserted road. They trudged a short distance through the waist-high dried grasses to an inlet where the water sparkled out toward the bay. Ducks paddled near the opposite bank, and the field on the other side was black and dense with honking Canadian geese. Guy stopped, put his hands on his hips. "This is great!"

"You come here often?" she asked.

"Used to, every fall. Just something about those honkers that I like. This is the flyway. They pass through here on their way south. Stop off to beef up a little before flying on."

She and Rolls didn't usually do things like this. They mostly spent their weekends raking leaves or going to a movie or a museum. This outdoorsy stuff was too much for her to plan and execute. She put her arm around Rolls, glad they could enjoy this together, glad at how easy Guy had made it for her.

Guy spread out the blanket and passed around the sandwiches. The sun was steady and warm. They ended up taking off their coats, as Guy had predicted. He handed the binocu-lars to Rolls, who stood and focused across the inlet.

"I used to come here a couple of times each fall. It's not crowded getting across the bridge this time of year. Weather can be real nice, like today," he said, opening a can of beer for Danny. He took out Cokes for himself and Rolls.

"Beer?" she said.

"You want a Coke instead?"

"No, thanks," she said, touched that he had specially brought the beer for her.

"We aim to please." He bit into his sandwich.

"Must be thousands of them," Rolls said. "Take a look, Mom."

Danny stood up and gazed across the inlet. The ground was covered with the gray bodies and tall black necks of thousands of geese preening or grazing in the field—a huge temporary society.

"Hunter's dream, huh?" Guy said.

"You can shoot them?"

"Sure you can, during the season. You can't shoot 'em when they're on the ground, though. And some of these places around here are parklands. You can't shoot 'em off parklands, either."

"Do people eat them?"

"They don't hang their heads up as trophies on their walls."

She laughed at the thought.

"You ever been hunting, Rolls?" Guy asked.

"No," Rolls answered, a little shocked at the question. He glanced at Danny. His look said, No one has ever thought I could do anything like that before.

"Do you hunt?" Danny asked.

"Years ago. Can't own a gun now. But, hey, I saw a sign for

a skeet shoot back in Easton. Should we go back there later? Try it out? Just for the fun of it?"

"I don't know . . ." Danny started.

"It's a living video game," Guy said to Rolls.

Rolls answered. "Okay. Sure."

Then Danny thought it might be all right between Guy and Rolls after all. They ate and Rolls wandered off with the binoculars. Danny, sleepy from the beer and the sun and the fresh air, lay back on the blanket with a sigh. "This is the most relaxed I've been in weeks. It's great!"

Guy stretched out beside her. "Yes, ma'am." He took her hand, stroked it. Just that much started a sweet ache. She closed her eyes and smiled, enjoying the old, familiar sensations that she'd been missing so long.

Then he rolled over to face her and held her hand in both of his. "You know Cheryl doesn't mean that much to me. Honestly."

His admission took her off guard. She thought she wanted Guy, but she wasn't sure for what. With Cheryl in Guy's life, Danny felt safer, even though she'd been jealous at first.

Her ego was involved. She had to try to be charming in ways that she hadn't practiced in years, had to mold herself into the interests and conversations of this man without compromising her interests and accomplishments. But what she wanted the most, she thought, was to sleep with him.

His body was wiry, tight and muscled right down to his cowboy boots. His blue eyes were expressive and honest. His face was tanned, and he'd earned the lines there—hard work and hard times. They gave him character.

He wasn't like the men she usually associated with—other teachers, Heck, the fathers of Rolls's friends. He wasn't smooth with words. In fact, talk frequently got him in trouble—the obscene comments, his going on about Cheryl.

He said what he thought. He didn't use euphemisms or skirt issues. That was refreshing in its own way. She felt he never hedged or lied to her.

But she wanted to go slowly. Her eyes still closed against the startling sunlight, she said, "I guess you and Cheryl still have some things to work out."

"I guess so. But goddammit, what I'm trying to say is, don't let her get in the way of us."

"Us?" She shaded her eyes and looked at him. "We've been out together exactly one time. Today."

"And we rode to work together every day for almost three months. I miss seeing you like that. I'd like to see you more often."

That was nice to hear. She faced the sky, feeling good about him. She also felt a little sorry for him, in her usual teacherly way. When he'd told her about his prison time, about the program and how he'd screwed up, she'd felt challenged in her tirelessly meddling way, to help, to see what gem she could form from this clay. And now, if he was really trying to break off from Cheryl, Danny thought she would be glad to be the one he could come to.

"So, when's a good time?" she asked.

"How about tomorrow night?" he suggested.

"No. Scouts' Thanksgiving dinner. They always hold it the Sunday before."

"I could see you Wednesday, but the next day's Thanksgiving. Don't you have to defrost the bird and fix the stuffing and all that?"

"Rolls hates turkey. We go Chinese. Peking duck. It's a lot easier."

Guy kissed her cheek. "It's a date, then."

The skeet shoot was a big party. Beer was sold out of kegs

sitting in tubs full of ice. Smoke from the chicken barbecuing in oil-drum halves wafted through the crowd.

"I wish we hadn't already eaten," Guy said. "That stuff smells great."

He held her hand easily as they wandered around the grounds. Rolls had gone ahead to the fenced area behind which the shooting took place.

The air crackled with the sounds of the skeet being launched from the trap, the burst of shots that blew it apart. A little further away, a turkey shoot was under way. A truck-load of birds in open wire cages sat in the field near the straw barrier. She could hear the high-pitched gobbles.

A country-western band was warming up on a flatbed truck at the end farthest from the turkeys. Both as a gesture of con-ciliation to Guy and to get away from the distressed gobbles, she steered them toward the music. Danny couldn't stand the twang, but she had to admit that the lyrics caught her attention—ballads about heartbreak, horses and women.

"How old do you have to be to shoot skeets?" Rolls asked.

"Old enough to slap your money on the table. Come on," said Guy.

Danny watched from a distance as Guy instructed Rolls in loading and aiming. He gestured to the trap and the man con-trolling it. He drew an arc in the sky with his arm. Then he stood behind Rolls and with his arms around her son, helped position the rifle.

Danny hoped Rolls's reflexes were good enough that he could hit the skeet. But even if he didn't, wasn't this man-to-man help and instruction part of what Rolls needed? Guy liked kids. She appreciated what he was doing.

The skeet flew. Rolls fired. The recoil surprised him, so he only fired once before the skeet fell. But he grinned at Guy, then hurried to reload and put Guy's instruction to immediate use. Danny knew he'd be determined not to let the kick distract him this time. He shot at the skeet several more times, never hitting it.

Then Guy paid. He loaded quickly, expertly, while Rolls watched in admiration. After he signaled the controller with a nod, he sighted and fired. The skeet exploded on the first shot. Rolls and Guy cheered. He fired once more and hit it again. Sensitive to Rolls, not wanting to show off too much, Guy lay the gun down and they strode back to her.

"Guy hit it first time both times," Rolls said.

"You made a damned good effort," Guy said to Rolls. "Just takes practice." Guy raised his head like he was sniffing the air. "Wanna shoot a turkey?"

"A live turkey?"

"Sure. It's not a real hunt. But it's fun. You get to take the turkey home."

"All shot up and bloody?" Danny asked in alarm.

"They'll clean it if you want."

"Rolls doesn't even like turkey."

"Then I'll take it home," Guy said. "What do you say?"

"I don't think I could hit it," Rolls answered miserably.

"You could try. Turkeys aren't as fast as skeets. It'd be good practice."

"What if I just wounded it? I'd hate for it to suffer," said Rolls.

Guy threw his arm over Rolls's shoulder. "Aw, come on. Turkeys are the dumbest birds on earth. Besides, I'll finish it off if you don't."

Danny glowered at him.

Guy glowered back. "Hell, it's a charity shoot. The profit goes to the church."

He and Rolls took off, walking fast toward the roped-off area.

"Shit!" Danny said aloud. There was a vast difference between doing outdoorsy, masculine things and torturing dumb birds. She was amazed at how dramatically and quickly her emotions shifted when it came to Guy Tomblin. At the moment, she hated him.

She made her way to the bake-sale table, and bought a large chocolate chip cookie, which she ate leaning against a fence post. In the distance, she could see full-feathered white turkeys being handed down from the truck. Several of them darted across the field. Shots rang out. As if in slow motion, one pure white turkey stumbled, spread its wings as if to fly, then cartwheeled over its wings twice before it landed dead.

Feeling sick, she returned to the truck and crawled into the seat.

Why did Guy have to do this, she wondered, when the day had been so perfect?

They were too different, she concluded. That's why she had all the emotional swings. They came from different backgrounds, had led different lives, held different values. He was barely educated and a criminal at that. She couldn't go on with him. It was ridiculous.

Rolls and Guy emerged from the crowd. Guy carried a big white garbage bag. She could see the blood through the plastic. He put it in the back of the truck while Rolls climbed in next to her.

"Well, how was it?" she asked her son.

Rolls raised his eyebrows. "Different."

"Did you shoot it?" she said as Guy got in and started the truck.

"No, I didn't try. Guy hit it with a single shot. I don't think the turkey felt a thing."

Guy backed the truck up. He was quiet, waiting, she knew, for her to say something first.

"Well, you'll have turkey for your table on Thursday," she said. "Cheryl and her roommate will be glad, I'm sure."

He corrected the angle of the rearview mirror. "Nah. I want to give it to that Latino kid at Grant—Romirez. You wanna take it to him for me?"

"Not me!"

He laughed and patted her leg. "Didn't think you would."

Cirri

CIRRI PUT HER HAIR UP, THE
way that Marcus liked. He had left early to go home to Mimi's
for a shower and clean clothes. They were to meet later at
school. She was just getting Pea and Willie up when Mama
stumbled in, coughing. She went straight into the bed and
curled up like a baby.

Pea clamored after her, "Mama! Hey, Mama!"

Willie said, "You all right, Mama?"

Mama didn't open an eye, just pulled the blanket closer up
under her chin and shivered.

"I'm getting her our blanket," Willie said and dashed off.
He came back with the blanket that he and Pea shared on the
couch. The two of them spread it carefully over Mama and
tucked it around her.

"That better?" Pea asked.

Mama couldn't stop coughing. Her chest sounded full and her nose was running, but she didn't wipe it.

Cirri was worried about Mama, but she was also angry. She left the room and hurried to fix peanut-butter-and-jelly sandwiches and to wash cereal bowls for breakfast.

She had told Mama to dress more warmly. She had told her to eat better. She had told her to get off the stuff. But now Mama was sick and, in a way, it was Cirri's fault. She liked going to school—the routines, the assignments, being with Marcus, feeling like she was going somewhere, doing something right and important. But she should have known that Mama was like a baby who needed to be taken care of.

Cirri jerked the barrette out of her hairdo and shook out the style. She wouldn't be going to school today.

"Come get your breakfast!" she yelled to the kids.

Willie came in first. "She's still shivering," he said somberly. "Why she so cold?"

"Been outside too long, I guess."

"No! It's 'cause she's sick!" He began to cry. "Her nose is runnin' and she's coughin'. I don't want Mama to be sick."

Cirri picked up the towel and flung it into Willie's lap. "Wipe's your face. And stop it. That's why I'm staying home with her today. Gonna feed her up right and get her warm. She be fine."

"What about school?"

"What about it?"

Pea came in. "Mama smells."

"Eat your breakfast," Cirri said.

"She do!"

Cirri ignored her and went on stuffing the sandwiches in brown bags, dropping two cookies in each.

"Cirri's stayin' with Mama today," Willie told Pea. "She'll take care of her."

"You're late now. Hurry up! If you miss that bus, I'm gonna wear you out," Cirri snapped.

After the kids left, Cirri ran the hottest water she could get into the bathtub and kept the door closed, so the room would fill up with steam. She remembered that when she was little and had a cough, Mama would keep a vaporizer going in the bedroom. They didn't have a vaporizer anymore, but she thought a bath and the steam would do Mama good. Mama wasn't sleeping, Cirri knew, because she was coughing every few seconds.

When the tub was ready and the bathroom was hot, Cirri took a deep breath and went into the bedroom where Mama lay, shivering. It was going to be hard work getting her to move.

"Mama," she said loudly. "I'm gonna put you in the bathtub now. Get up."

This close, Cirri realized that Pea was right. Mama did smell. She pulled the blankets off, exposing Mama's dirty coat, her bare legs, and aqua house slippers. "Come on, Mama. I'm taking you someplace nice and warm."

Mama didn't open her eyes. "Gimme that blanket," she said curling herself tighter into a ball.

Cirri took Mama's wrists and pulled her up. Mama kept her arms tucked in close to her chest, but she was light and couldn't resist any more than that. Cirri pulled her to her feet, and Mama fell against her.

"Leave me alone," Mama mumbled.

Cirri pulled her, struggling, into the heat of the bathroom where Mama collapsed onto the cold floor. Cirri closed the door to keep in the steam and quickly stripped off Mama's coat and dress. Mama didn't resist; she was bent double coughing.

The stench made Cirri gag.

She tossed the filthy clothes out of the room and pulled Mama up again. Mama was shivering so much now, she seemed to have no control over her muscles. Her arms jerked, her head bobbed, her teeth were clacking.

"Get in!" Cirri ordered and helped Mama lift a leg into the tub.

"It's hot," Mama cried.

"I know. Get in," Cirri said, almost in tears herself.

"Why you doin' this to me, Cirri? Please! Please!" Mama sobbed as she sank into the water.

But once the hot water covered her and the steam rose up into her face, she seemed to relax, though the coughing continued.

Cirri sat back on her heels and stared at Mama. She was as skinny as the starving kids in Africa that Cirri had seen pictures of in the newspaper. Her hip bones jutted out and her ribs were visible under the skin. No meat at all. But her wrists and hands, her ankles and feet were swollen. Her breasts were shriveled-up bags hanging close to her armpits. Everywhere—on her arms, her thighs, her hands, her neck—there were scars along the veins. Some were old scars, healed over and shiny. Some were fresh ones that seemed to bother her in the hot water, because she rubbed at them.

Cirri remembered Mama when she used to dress up to go to work in her nice blouses and heels, perfume, makeup and earrings. She would hurry around the apartment in the morning in her stockings and slip, reminding Cirri about this or that for school, feeding Pea in her high chair, and teasing with Willie. Daddy was gone sometimes then, but they still did fine. She was a secretary at the Department of the Interior, and Mrs. Robertson took care of the kids. Mama would put Cirri on the bus to school, then go on to work.

Now Mama looked grotesque, with her lips pulled back and

her teeth chattering, her eyes sunken in and her hair full of lint.

Maybe if she fixed Mama up—washed her hair, soaped her all over, dressed her in clean, warm clothes and gave her a decent meal—Mama would mend. And, if she saw herself like she used to be, wouldn't she want to stay off the stuff? Wouldn't she give it up?

Cirri wet Mama's hair and poured on what little was left of the shampoo. Mama groaned. Her shoulders and arms started to jerk again, but Cirri kept at it, washing the filthy, stiff hair until it felt soft again and smelled good. Then she made Mama sit up while she washed her back and chest and underarms. She squeezed the warm water onto Mama to rinse her.

Mama held her head like it was hurting her. Snot dropped into the water. Cirri jerked Mama up and made her stand while she washed the rest of her. The tub was oily and gray by the time the bath was over. She helped Mama out of the tub and threw one towel around her and another one over her head.

"Hold on to me," she said, afraid that Mama might fall because she was shaking so badly. Mama clutched at her while Cirri lowered Mama onto the toilet seat. "Sit here. I'm gonna get some clothes."

She ran to get her favorite pale pink sweat suit. She hardly ever wore it because she liked to keep it nice, but it was the warmest thing she could think of.

When she returned to the bathroom, Mama was coughing up horrible-smelling green stuff into the sink. Cirri ran the water to wash it away. Then she helped Mama into the clothes and led her into the kitchen. She sat her down at the table and wrapped the two blankets around her. She dried Mama's hair, then parted it and brushed it as well as she could, but it was

full of knots. She gave up after a while, when Mama's head fell
forward.

Cirri bent down to her. "What, Mama?"

"Don't bother me no more."

Cirri put the brush down. "I'm gonna make you some
eggs."

Mama laid her head on the table, still breathing hard and
coughing.

Cirri knew that Mama needed medicine, but maybe the
food would help some. Maybe if she'd get some good food in
her stomach and go to sleep, she'd wake up feeling better. But
what about her breathing? The steam hadn't helped. There
was a noisy scratch in Mama's chest. And there was the green
slime in the sink that she had coughed up. What kind of medicine did she need? And how could Cirri pay for it?

She stirred the eggs and heated some milk in a small pan.
When Cirri was sick as a little girl, Mama would give her
warm milk, and it always tasted so good. Warm milk and
homemade oatmeal and raisin cookies. Mama would prop
Cirri up with pillows in Mama and Daddy's own bed and read
books to her, or color in a coloring book with her. Mama
would color one page and Cirri would color the other. Mama's
pictures were always so neat and bright with lavenders and or-
anges and greens. When Cirri tired of coloring, Mama would
get out the cards and they would play Fish or War or some
other game until Cirri got sleepy. Then Mama would settle
Cirri deep under the covers and rub her forehead until she
went to sleep.

Daddy would come home at dinnertime and want to know
how his sick baby was. Then they would all three sit on the
bed with Cirri between them to watch the evening TV shows.
Mama would bring them trays of dinner, and warm milk for

Cirri. Daddy would feel her forehead with his big, heavy hand and put his arm around her so that she was hugged in close. "Her head still feels hot," he would say to Mama. "Your throat hurting you?" he would ask Cirri. And then they would discuss appointment times and clinics and medicines. But mostly what Cirri remembered was his thick, comforting arm around her and the concern in his voice, the fun she'd had with Mama all day, and the warm milk.

Cirri studied Mama. She appeared to be asleep, except that every few seconds she coughed or twitched. What about Mama's friends, all those folks she partied with? Surely they must know she was sick. Would they pitch in some money so Cirri could take Mama to the clinic where a doctor would give her the right medicine? But when she thought about it more, she figured those people didn't care about Mama or they never would have let her get this bad off. Probably they were all this bad off themselves. She thought about Thea, but she knew that the bank was pretty much empty. She knew Marcus would give her the money without batting an eye. But the more she asked for, the more he would have to work.

She put the food down in front of Mama and gently shook her. "Look, Mama, I got something for you here. Sit up and I'll give you some of this."

Mama raised her head and looked at the food with disgust.

"Come on. You gonna eat some of this. Get something in your stomach. Get up your strength." Cirri held up a forkful and Mama opened her mouth. It took a long time, but gradually she ate all of it. Then she started coughing and couldn't stop, and soon all the food had come up again and was splattered all over on the floor. The kitten, who had been out of sight till then, came nosing around. Cirri kicked it away, screaming, "Get out of here! Get out!"

* * *

Mama slept for a while. She woke up twitching so much it felt as if an earthquake were happening on the bed. "Cirri, I'm so tired," she groaned.

"Go back to sleep, then," Cirri mumbled, exhausted and angry.

"Can't. I needs the stuff. See me? See this?" She held up one quivering arm.

Cirri turned away.

"Cirri," Mama shrieked. "There's a hustler down the corner. Wears a blue coat and hat. Tell him I need it now. 'S been too long."

"I'm not going down there," Cirri said.

"He'll say he not gonna give me any. I owe him. Too much. But tell him I'll get it to him. I swear. Tonight."

"Where's this money coming from?"

"I swear! Tell him. I need it now!"

"You don't need nothing but to get well," Cirri said.

"I be fine after that."

"Fine for a couple hours. I'm not going nowhere."

"Cirri, please," Mama pleaded.

Cirri left the room and went to stare at the TV. When she checked on Mama after *I Love Lucy*, Mama was gone. She took the cat onto her lap and watched the shows. There was nothing else she could do.

An hour later, the door slammed. She found Mama in the kitchen fooling with a needle against her leg. The pink sweat suit was wet and black with grime down one side. Mama's face was skinned up and bloody. She grinned. "Roughed me up a little, but he give it to me. Give me plenty. I'm gonna be fine."

Cirri wasn't even angry. Somehow she had known this would happen. She sat down and watched Mama, the needle, the bead of blood. Then Mama sat back and closed her eyes. She coughed, but the jerking and twitching slowed.

"Cirri, come with me."

"I'm not going nowhere."

"An' we don't even have to leave out this kitchen." She lifted a small plastic bag. "I got some extra stuff. You'll like it."

Cirri didn't say anything. There was nothing she could do and no one she could go to for help.

"I want to take you there just once so you can see why I go. I don't want you to hate me, Cirri. I named you after the clouds. I loved you so much when you were little, I thought my heart would break of loving you so much. You take such good care a' me, baby. I wanna show you the clouds."

Cirri wanted to cry, hearing Mama talk like this. She loved Mama too, but they had nothing but problems now, and it seemed like there was no way out. So Cirri held out her arm, and Mama gave her what was left in the needle.

That was how Marcus found them, sitting there, the needle on the table between them. Cirri felt like she was floating, like Mama had said. They were floating together, holding hands. And Mama looked fine. In some distant place, she still coughed and breathed hard, but up in the air, floating, she looked beautiful again, the sweet Mama of the warm milk and glowing colored pictures.

Cirri was glad to see Marcus. Everything suddenly seemed open and fine. Blue skies. She got up and kissed him, but he held her away from him.

"Why didn't you come to school?"

"School?" Cirri wondered vaguely what time it was, but it didn't seem important.

"I left school 'cause I was worried about you. How long you been doing this?"

Again, time eluded her.

He jerked her toward him. "You hooked? I told you *never* to fool with shit." He screamed and squeezed her arms till they hurt. "Didn't I tell you?"

She shrugged. "It's okay, baby."

"It's *not* okay."

"Don't hurt her," Mama said weakly. "But it always does come to hurt."

"Why you do this, Cirri?" Marcus's face curled up as he held in tears. "Why you mess us all up?"

Then he ran out and slammed the door. It sounded to Cirri like thunder in the clouds.

Mama didn't leave as she usually did in the afternoons. She went to sleep instead. She was so sweaty that Cirri figured she had a fever. For an hour or more, Cirri sat on the bed and watched her, wanting to stay close like they were when they were floating.

She remembered the floating, the clouds Mama had told her would be there. But then Marcus had come and the clouds had turned mean. She was mad at Marcus because he was mad at her. She had put her head down on the table and cried. Mama had comforted her. "Poor baby," she had said. "Menfolks never understand the trouble we go through for them. Don't never appreciate it."

Soon the kids were pounding on the door. "You didn't meet us," they screamed. "Where you been? We had to walk home by ourselves. Past all them hustlers."

"I was here with Mama," Cirri answered quietly.

"Mama's here!" Pea shouted.

"Yeah, but she's 'sleep. An' she needs her sleep. So don't go bothering her," she said, shushing them.

"She still sick?" Willie asked.

" 'Course she is. Don't get all well in a few hours when you're sick."

"Does she still smell?" Pea wanted to know.

"No, she had a bath."

That seemed to satisfy them.

The three of them watched TV as the drug drained out of Cirri's system. She felt weak, and she kept remembering Marcus and the door slamming. He had walked out on her. When everything had been so sweet, he had squeezed her arms until he hurt her. He had yelled at her and told her she had messed it all up.

She grabbed the kitten as it tiptoed passed her and forced it to sit on her lap. She stroked it and watched TV with unseeing eyes. He had left her.

Mama was too sick to go out that night. Cirri slept next to her, feeling Mama shake the bed with her coughs and shivering. Sometime in the night, she heard Mama get up, heard her in the kitchen, heard something fall into the sink.

In the morning Cirri found the needle in the sink. She hid it in a cupboard away from the kids.

After she put them on the bus, she walked to Thea's house. She didn't know what else to do. Mama was still in bed, still feverish, still coughing. There was no point in going to school. It was the day before Thanksgiving. No one would be doing any work anyway. Besides, she needed to talk to Thea.

Thea's house smelled of cinnamon-baked apples, onions, bacon, greens. Bryan sat in the infant seat waving his arms and gurgling. Thea, in her pink nightgown, hurried around the kitchen mixing up the ingredients for pumpkin pie.

"Don't be asking me for no money, girl!" Thea exclaimed.

"You know I ain't got none. You and me done cleaned out that bank. And the day they find out, um, um, um."

On the way to Thea's, Cirri had seen a money machine that said Cirrus. It struck her strange that it could bear her name and have all those twenty-dollar bills stacked inside it, and she couldn't get a one.

"Mama's bad sick," she said.

Thea cracked eggs into the bowl. "Uh huh. I know what she sick with. Been telling you that for a long time."

Cirri didn't need a lecture. "She's got some kinda cold and a cough. She can't hardly breathe. That don't have nothing to do with the other thing."

"Strung-out folks don't take care of themselves. Only care about getting that next fix," said Thea.

Cirri's mouth watered as she smelled the spices and saw the fresh-baked bread on the counter and the turkey defrosting in the sink.

"And we not gonna have any kind of Thanksgiving," Cirri said. Then her voice caught and she put a hand over her eyes, trying not to cry.

Thea looked at her. "This not like you, Cirri. Whatsa matter?"

Cirri let the tears come. She had no choice. "Marcus left me."

Thea stooped down so Cirri could cry against her. "He ain't no good."

"He was good to me."

She nodded toward Bryan. "That's child's father was good to me, too."

"I wish I was pregnant. Maybe he wouldn't of left. Maybe he'd still care."

"Only male caring about me right now is that one." Thea jerked her head toward Bryan again. "He caring about wanting me to feed him and wipe his little be-hind. That what you want?"

"At least I'd have a little part of Marcus."

"Yep. The part any man leaves is microscopic. All the rest we take care of for eighteen years."

Cirri pulled away. "Stop it!"

Thea stood up and returned to her batter. "He say goodbye?"

"We had a falling out."

"A fight?"

"Not a fight."

" 'Bout what?"

Cirri scowled. "I don't feel like getting into it."

Thea stirred the pumpkin. "Fine time to leave you, with your Mama sick and Thanksgiving here. He a conceited, thoughtless bastard. That's what he is. Honestly, chile, you lucky to be rid of him. I know you don't feel that right now. But you are," she said.

"No. I'm the one let *him* down."

"Uh huh. You still got it bad. Ain't hit you yet."

"I'm gonna get him back." For the first time, it had occurred to her that maybe she could. He had acted like he cared for her. He had said they would move in together someday. How could all that vanish so fast? How could he throw all that away because of one mistake? People made mistakes all the time. Maybe he was missing her and was thinking he would forgive her if she swore never to fool with the stuff again. She would swear. She would never go near it again, if only he would come back.

". . . I know it'd be okay with my folks," Thea was saying.

"What?"

"You listening?"

"No."

Thea laughed at Cirri's honesty. "I said, Give yourself a couple days off from him. Then you'll see you don't need him like you think you do. Come here tomorrow for Thanksgiving. I know it'd be okay with my folks. We got plenty food. No sense you and them kids sitting over there without no dinner. An' over here nobody gonna let you even *think* about no Marcus Chance."

Cirri looked at the kitchen clock. If she hurried, she could get over to school and maybe see Marcus before she had to meet the kids. She stood up and smoothed her hair. She hadn't fixed it this morning and now she was sorry.

"So?" Thea demanded.

"I'm going."

Thea planted her hands on her hips. "You comin' tomorrow?"

Cirri looked at her, unsure.

"You were just sittin' here cryin' about no Thanksgiving dinner. Well, I'm offerin' you one."

Cirri couldn't plan beyond the next hour. What if they did get back together? What if he invited her to dinner at Mimi's? Surely, Mimi would be having a Thanksgiving dinner. What if he gave her money for Mama? And she could take Mama to the doctor. All of a sudden there were too many possibilities.

"Can I tell you tomorrow?"

"Now you gonna go chasin' him, ain't you?"

Cirri nodded and grinned. It was a terrific idea. Didn't he always say he had to be chasing after her? Now she would show him exactly how much she cared by going after him.

Thea looked skyward. "Lord help her, 'cause she surely can't help herself."

"I got to." Cirri headed for the door.

"Wait!" Thea ran down the hall and returned with a brown bottle. "Cough medicine."

Cirri fled. She ran all the way to the bus stop, but the buses were slow at this time of day. It was ten or twelve blocks to school. She started running.

There was a long uphill several blocks before school. She had to slow down, bend over and pull in air. But as soon as she felt better, she started to jog again.

All the while she imagined him in the corridor, trudging to class with everyone else, imagined how she would surprise him from behind, grab his hand and pull him aside. "I made a big mistake, baby. I know I did. But Mama was sick . . . Don't do this to us because of one mistake. Everyone makes mistakes. I ran all the way here. I came to you, Marcus. Not playin' hard to get. You got me, dahlin'. If you'll have me."

She could see his silly grin, feel the solid weight of his arm drop across her shoulders. She knew he'd say something stupid like, "Love's our drug." Or, "Now we got something to be thankful for tomorrow."

Lots of kids were out on the sidewalk in front of C & J's, drinking sodas, smoking, sharing fries, talking. She was across the street and walking fast—only one more block to school—when she saw him come out of C & J's and hold the door. Tina Jasper followed him. They leaned against the wall. He offered her some fries and she helped herself. Marcus was having a good ol' time. He touched Tina's arm, telling some grand story.

Cirri thought of the bottle in her pocket. Broken, it could do a nice job of messin' up her face, the principal's daughter who thought she owned the world. Now it looked like she had Marcus, too.

The door opened again and Nick Tiebault emerged. He joined them—ugly white hustler with a single little earring and his coat collar turned up. If it wasn't for him, Marcus wouldn't be in the business, working nights, getting in deeper and deeper. She wanted to gouge out his eyes. He gave Tina a smoke and lit it for her.

Cirri fingered the bottle. They would never know what hit them. She could do her business, see the blood fly, then be gone.

Nick and Marcus were talking to each other. Tina was dragging on that cigarette. Cirri stepped behind a telephone pole. She wanted to hurt them all, leave them in as much pain as she was feeling. She leaned against the pole, turned her back on them and stared at the school.

It looked like a prison perched up on top of the hill with the grills over its windows and the dirty redbrick walls so straight and square and unyielding. But as she thought ahead to the stretch of four days with nowhere to go, with Mama sick and the kids with no Thanksgiving dinner and her with no future at all, the prison of a school looked pretty good.

A bell rang, signaling the change of periods. Someone was laughing over at C & J's. She turned to look. Marcus, Tina and Nick were gone. She studied the bottle in her hand. Mama needed it. Time to go home.

Danny

DANNY SPOTTED TROUBLE when Johnny Lucas sprinted into the room between classes and took a seat. He never came early to class. He rarely ever came to school.

"Eager to get here?" she asked him.

He yelped nervously and beat on the top of the desk as if it were a set of bongos.

When she heard the noise in the hallway, she stepped out to investigate. T-man, football-player-size, was storming toward her, fists clenched. He was flanked by girls, some pleading with him to stop, others shrieking encouragement. Anya dragged along behind. Danny didn't know what was up, but she knew she would need help.

She shouted to Anya. "Run next door! Have the teacher call security!" Then she straight-armed T-man. "What's this all about?"

"Johnny been seeing Claudine on the sly," one girl shouted.

"Claudine and T-man been going together two months."

"You call that going together? He does what he wants. Why can't she?"

T-man snarled to Danny, "It's none of your business."

Danny knew she had to keep T-man from getting into the classroom. "You're not moving till security comes. Then you're going to the office."

He grabbed her wrist. "Get out my way."

Johnny called from inside, standing behind Danny, fists raised. "Come on, motha-fuck."

T-man shoved past Danny and lunged at Johnny. Desks flew, the girls wailed. The boys grabbed each other and stumbled around the room in an odd embrace, grunting. Johnny's nose began to pour blood. T-man tripped and fell backwards, landing on an upended desk with Johnny on top of him. He yowled in pain. Teachers and students from other classes rushed in. Danny tried to contain the girls until security arrived and pulled the boys apart.

The assistant principal came to cover Danny's class, while she went to the office to make her report. T-man was in with Heck and security. Two policemen were in the outer office in case they were needed, but this was Heck's jurisdiction. Johnny sat on the chairs, an ice pack on his nose.

When she walked into Heck's office, two security yellow jackets were holding T-man's arms behind him. "Claudine Boucher!" he was yelling.

Heck bellowed back, "And you got to mash Johnny's nose across his face because of her?"

"Damn straight!"

"I suspended you a week and a half ago. You're not even supposed to be in this building."

"I got a right."

"You know the rules."

His brows were lowered over his eyes in fierceness. "I can do anything I goddamn want."

"Where's your mother? Where's your father? Before you set foot in this building they have to come and ask me, Can you *please* come back in."

"Nobody gonna come beggin' to you."

"Your uncle have keys to get into school buildings?" Heck demanded.

T-man missed a beat and squinted at Heck. "What if he do?"

"You and Claudine come in here last week, into this office?"

"What you talkin' 'bout?"

"Came in here and busted up every pane of glass?"

T-man laughed.

"Ate some fries and fucked on my desk?"

He was fierce and stubborn again. "Yeah. Go prove it, man. Knock yourself out."

"Trespassing," Heck ticked off the charges. "Destruction of public property, thousands of dollars' worth of damage rifling through private documents. And now"—he pointed toward the outer office where Johnny sat—"assault, more destruction. I could send you up for a long time."

"The fuck you can."

"Get down on your knees," Heck growled.

"Make me."

Heck nodded to the yellow jackets and they bent T-man's arms until he knelt.

Heck paced around him. "Get used to it, Theodore, 'cause the police are gonna have you in this position an awful lotta the time."

"What you . . ."

"No! You listen! Shut your goddamned mouth and listen!

You like beatin' up people, bustin' up things? Show you're a big man? Everybody gotta watch out?" Heck stopped in front of T-man, and Danny thought he was going to spit on him. "I'll tell you something. You're nothing. That's what. Nothing!"

Danny felt uncomfortable. Heck was tough with kids. He needed to be. But now he was letting his personal stuff blind him. She wondered if she should interrupt him.

"You hang on the street corners talking a lot of jive and you fuck a lot of girls and you smoke shit and you think you living. Well, you ain't!" Heck shouted. "You hear that? You're nothin'!"

He leaned wearily against his desk, and said, "Let's get this over with. Were you and Claudine in here last Tuesday?"

T-man raised his head. "Fuck you, Jasper."

Another class was about to start. Danny hurried to her room and gave the new class the reading assignment. Then she sat down to think while they skimmed the pages.

Heck had gone too far. This upset her more than the fight. The pitiful, desperate hostility of the kids was beginning to get to him. Too many years on the front lines. She couldn't blame him. He was one in a million, but even men like him could lose their good judgment.

She walked to the window and located the monuments as a means of distraction. It would take hours for her to calm down. Even if T-man had, in fact, ransacked Heck's office, Heck was taking the attack too personally. Yet he *would* take it personally because that was how he ran the school. He wasn't content to be a symbol of authority. He wanted to be *the* authority, *the* father for these kids. That was the way he'd always played it. So naturally, such an attack would hurt even more.

She assigned this class little homework. They wouldn't do it anyway. Instead, they worked here. Under her nose, they managed to get a half hour or forty minutes of work done a day. It was the best she could expect from them. Twelve were absent.

One girl who had finished reading put her head down on her desk to sleep. Another took out her hairbrush. Danny got up and strolled over to them. She patted the tired girl on the back. "We're going to talk about this in a minute. Stay with us," she said quietly.

She felt sorry for them. None of these kids was bad. Yes, she had to struggle to keep them interested. They got out of hand now and then. They made D's and F's. They dragged down Dr. Canaletti's test scores. But, when all was said and done, they were just kids. They trusted people. They trusted the school system and the government. They had goals way beyond what any of them would ever achieve. One wanted to play pro ball, another said she wanted to be a heart surgeon, a third was going to be a criminal lawyer and make a lot of money. They believed that they would reach those goals, and that everything would come out all right.

What they didn't know was the reality. All the adults they trusted had already given up on them. She had heard their parents say, "When my kids reach twelve, fourteen, I tell 'em they got to make their own way." Too many teachers said, "Baby-sit. That's what I do."

It depressed her because they deserved more. There was still hope and possibility for them, if anyone took the time. Even when T-man was storming down the hall toward her, she knew she could try to stop him, try to talk to him. He wouldn't hurt her, because he wasn't essentially malevolent or malicious. He really hoped that someone would appeal to his better side, that an adult could and would take control, help him choose the best way out of a tough situation.

These kids thought they were ready for the world, but they

weren't. They had nothing going for them. Most people had already betrayed them.

Anya was waiting for Danny in the hall outside of her office at lunchtime. Danny was in a rush and did not feel like hearing about the latest Cooper family feud. "Can it wait until later?" she asked. "This has been quite a day."

"I called security for you," Anya reminded her.

"I know." Danny nodded and forced a smile.

"Is T-man going to jail?"

"I don't know."

"Dr. Jasper told me to talk to you."

"He did, did he?" said Danny, trying to hide her exasperation.

She dumped her books on her desk. When she turned to Anya, she was shocked to see the black eye. "How did that happen?"

"I walked into a door at home," Anya mumbled.

"A door? Anya, come on." Danny didn't need one more thing, but all of sudden she was concerned.

The girl looked down. "At night. When I got up to go to the bathroom."

Danny lifted Anya's chin and questioned her with a look.

"Dr. Jasper said I should come talk to you if there was anything about Miz Brown bothering me," Anya said, backing away.

Heck hadn't said anything, but then he frequently sent kids to her unannounced.

"Well, there is something bothering me," Anya continued.

"What?"

"Miz Brown gets real mad sometimes."

Danny crossed her arms.

"And yesterday she got in a fight with Nick Tiebault."

"A fight?"

"A yelling fight."

Danny was in no mood for more trouble today, and this story was spreading into places she didn't want to go. "You've heard yelling before," she said.

"This was different," Anya said stubbornly.

"What started it?"

"I don't know." Anya shrugged. "But all of a sudden Nick was up there calling her a ugly fat-assed bitch, and she was saying she was going to kill him."

"Kill him?"

Tears welled up in the girl's eyes, and then she was sobbing. "I think she wants to kill all the white kids. That's what my mother says."

Danny steered Anya to a chair, gave her a tissue, and knelt down in front of her. There was no evidence of a bruise on her forehead or cheek. The injury was just to the eye. Anya dabbed at it carefully.

"Anya," Danny asked gently. "How did your eye get hurt?"

"I walked into a door!"

"All right, I'll talk to Nick," Danny said with a sigh. "Tomorrow."

The next morning, first period, while the other kids were doing their five-minute warm-up, Danny told Nick to join her in the hall.

"Ooh, Nick-y," someone sang out.

"When he gonna do his work?" another student complained.

"When are you gonna do yours?" Danny countered.

Nick lounged against the corridor wall, his arms crossed.

"Don't get into it with Miz Brown," Danny said. "You know who'll win in that situation."

"Bitch is on my case. " 'M'I s'posed to sit there an' take it?" he asked defiantly.

"Just ignore her," Danny said, taking her own advice.

"Pretty hard to do when she's calling my name, making me stand up and be made a fucking example of."

"Take it easy," she warned him.

"No. I won't. You don't understand. I don't take shit from nobody. Someone crosses me, they pay. Simple as that." He was jabbing a finger at her and the words twisted his mouth.

She looked away down the hall trying to contain her temper. "Look, Nick, you're doing fine in school. Better than fine," she said.

"Shit, yes. I can do fine anywhere. I got brains and things going on nobody even dreams about. That's how smart I am."

"Great! So why blow it? Get outta here next year. Go on and use those brains and all this anger and drive . . ."

" 'Cause she's messin' with me."

"It's hard being in this school and being . . ."

He jabbed a finger at her. "She's talkin' about she wants to *kill* me. Do you believe that?"

"It's wrong . . ."

"She doesn't know who the fuck she's dealin' with. That's all I got to say." He jerked open the classroom door and strode back in.

Heck had been gone all day at a meeting, so Danny went to Miz Brown's room herself after school. She did not want a scene. The last time they'd had a little talk, they had ended up screaming at each other. The school had been treated to a lot of gossip fodder for a long time. The woman was so unreasonable that Danny didn't know how anyone could get along with her. Why didn't Heck make her tone down her diatribes?

Danny stood at the open door, not wanting to enter Miz Brown's room without an invitation. "Knock, knock," she said. Miz Brown glared at her. "Yes?"

Danny took a few steps into the room and decided on a light approach. She chuckled. "Anya Cooper was in my office crying today because she said you were going to kill Nick Tiebault. I told her she heard things wrong. . . ."

"I would like to."

"He's not my favorite kid, either. . . ."

"No! I really would like to," Miz Brown said, not smiling. "If I could find a way and not get caught."

"He's really gotten to you, huh?" Danny said, remembering kids she'd been mad at before. "What'd he do?"

"He is everything I mistrust. Everything I hate."

"He's not too pleasant. . . ."

"He's a devil," Miz Brown said flatly.

Danny felt a chill. This was more than one kid under her skin. "Because he's white?"

"Partly." Miz Brown looked out at the empty chairs as if the kids were there and she was considering each one. "But some of the black kids are just as bad. The black community is sick at heart and nobody listens to me. I don't trust any of them, to tell the truth."

"How do you get yourself to come here day after day?" Danny asked quietly, beginning to be afraid of what she was going to hear.

"It's my job."

"It's your job, but if you don't even like the kids, why . . . ?"

"More and more they scare me," Miz Brown admitted. "I've been teaching for sixteen years. I always felt I was telling the kids what they needed to know, and they appreciated that. Now, they're either up in my face, or else they don't take it seriously. They laugh." She shook her head. "They think they have all the answers. They have no idea what they're up against in this society."

"What's Nick's specific problem?"

"Are you here to defend him?"

"I'm just trying to understand why Anya was so upset."

"She has the brains of a worm."

"She's not very bright, but—"

"And Nick Tiebault has never spent two minutes in here listening to a thing I'm saying," Miz Brown interrupted, as if Danny's comments weren't worth listening to. "He's disrespectful and he has a superiority problem. A white-superiority problem."

Danny tried to contain her temper. "He's a cocky kid. It often comes with the age. You know that."

Miz Brown glared at her. "It always goes with the race."

Danny was determined not to get sidetracked. "When you are constantly provoking and berating the white students, constantly preaching hate, why are you surprised when it comes back at you?"

"I am not *preaching* anything. I am *teaching* reality. I am trying to educate students, black and white, about life in America. About its history of ongoing hate."

Danny could feel blood beginning to pound in her neck. She raised her voice. "The country has its problems. But what about your problems? You talk about hatred eight hours a day, five days a week. That's sickness! And I don't care what color you are."

Miz Brown drew herself up and sneered. "I am talking about truth."

"Bitter truth from a bitter person," Danny spat back.

"Why the hell do you think I'm bitter but because of jive-assed, opinionated honkies like you coming to tell me how to run my life?"

Danny took that in. Sweat stood on her forehead. She tried to regain her composure, lowered her voice. "Aren't you afraid? You insult people. You make people hate you back. Doesn't it scare you?" she hissed.

"No!" Miz Brown shouted. "Because I've got protection right here." She tapped her fingernails on her top drawer. "And, I swear, if Nick Tiebault had come an inch closer to me, I would have used it. I told him I would kill him. And I meant it."

Danny took a step back in disbelief. "What are you talking about?"

She held up a small desk key attached to her watch. "I have it under lock and key. But I'll use it if I need to."

Heck

EVERY MONTH CANALETTI AS-
sembled his district's principals, to communicate information
about the citywide spelling bee, about the Scholars in the
Schools program, about deadlines and evaluations. And there
were more complex things to discuss. Canaletti tried to devote
half of each meeting to brainstorming about a specific issue.
In the past, he had talked about curriculum requirements,
teacher performance, building maintenance, security problems, et cetera. Today's topic was PTA relations.

Heck thought it was a bunch of bull. Canaletti wouldn't
look at the real problems. The meetings were a whitewash.
He leaned back in his chair and stretched his aching legs as
the woman in charge of the spelling bee made her presentation, stating deadlines and offering suggestions for the teachers.

Heck couldn't focus. The past drew him away. He was

thinking about Charlemagne, who had given birth to an educational revolution. In 800 A.D., when the world now known as Europe slumbered in an existence of mud-soaked farms and a few disease-ridden villages, Charlemagne established a school at his palace in Aachen, where the best students and teachers in the empire were brought together. Heck imagined the thick, cold slabs of irregularly shaped stones of the floor of the palace. The walls rose stone upon stone packed with mud, with slits for windows. Animal skins hung on the walls to block drafts.

Down the corridor strode Charlemagne himself, an unusually tall man with shrewd eyes. At the age of sixty-three, he was still strong and alert. He did not wear the cloaks and elaborate crowns that befitted his status. He wore a simple rough wool tunic, leather pants and high boots. He was a man given less to symbol than to action.

His retinue consisted of military men because he was, foremost, a genius of war. The empire that he had put together extended from Italy and Spain to Denmark, from Germany to the Atlantic Ocean. He was the only one in the world's history to successfully control all this under one head.

Light came in from the high windows of the rooms where his school was housed. Monks and students hunched over ancient Roman manuscripts, some of which had been damaged by fire or insects or mold. Students were copying them to preserve the wisdom.

In other rooms students recited for their emperor and benefactor. Teachers bowed in gratitude. The training and culture they had received here would be spread throughout the Empire. The church would be strengthened. Learning would be revived.

"The Carolingian Renaissance," Heck said and smiled. He was pleased at having remembered the name. Carolingian minuscule was the style of handwriting used by the monks and students which later gave way to print type. So he said, "And Carolingian minuscule."

"You with us, Heck?" asked Florence Pepper, the principal from North, who'd been his friend for many years.

Canaletti was standing at the head of the table as he always did. "Approximate attendance at your last meeting?"

Heck blushed. What meeting was Canaletti talking about? "Sorry. I was a million miles away."

"Maybe not a million. Maybe just in Bermuda or some other place warm," Florence teased.

"I guess so," he said, grateful for her humor.

Everyone else nodded in support.

"Attendance at your last PTA meeting," Canaletti repeated.

Heck took a deep breath. Some part of him had heard the discussion about attendance. "At the end of our last PTA meeting we came out to see ambulance lights down the way. One of our students had been shot in the stairwell of his building. Sixteen years old. Dead."

"But what was the attendance?"

"He hadn't been in school much prior to that. And he wasn't a great student, needless to say. But he had one claim to fame. He drew great naked women. The kid was an artistic genius when it came to that. The proportions, the shadings. Everything was . . . I mean, just outstanding."

Canaletti sat down and drummed his fingers in impatience.

"Thirty-five or forty-five parents," Heck said. "Not many."

"Thank you, Dr. Jasper. When we're talking about parental involvement . . ." Canaletti began.

"Is that what we're talking about?" Heck asked.

Canaletti narrowed his eyes at him.

"Parental involvement is a whole different issue from PTA,"

Heck said. "We all know that. So why do you worry so much about attendance at PTA meetings?"

Canaletti said, "It's a *measure* of interest level."

"PTA means coming out at night into a risky neighborhood after a long day of work. It means sitting through a boring meeting primarily devoted to asking for money. Parents care about their kids, but PTA doesn't have a damn thing to do with it."

"If you care enough about your child's schooling, you can make it to a couple of meetings a year, it seems to me," Canaletti said, his voice rising. "Part of what we're here to talk about is how to make those meetings interesting so attendance will improve."

Heck idly scratched at a spot on the table. Canaletti and the others waited for his reply, but Heck said nothing.

"Well?" Canaletti finally prompted.

"I was just thinking about the kid's mother. She talked to me when she came to collect his things out of his locker. She worked two jobs. During the day she was a cashier at a car dealership, and in the evenings she cleaned offices. She wanted to get out of the building they lived in because she knew it wasn't good for Darnell. That's why she worked so hard. She came home that night to the neighbors telling her her son was dead."

"So you're saying that's why she couldn't come to the meeting."

Heck pounded the table. "No, goddammit. I'm saying there are more important things to talk about than the friggin' PTA."

"What do you suggest?" Canaletti yelled back. "Why didn't you have that kid in school every day? Why he was such a lousy student? Why was it that the only thing in the whole world he excelled in was pornography?"

"No!" Heck returned. "It wasn't pornography. It was like Greek or Roman art."

"Why wasn't he in school?" Canaletti demanded.

Heck felt like a venerable, wise ox resting in a field, and Canaletti was the fly buzzing around him. The fly would never understand the ox's perspective, but would continue to bother the ox until, at last, the ox would move, just to get away from the fly's stupid questions. "I don't know," Heck answered. "But *that* is the kind of issue we need to address."

"Why, once he was there, was he doing so poorly?"

Heck looked away, trying to remember Darnell, trying to frame an answer that Canaletti might understand. "He didn't put in any effort."

"His mother was putting in a lot of effort. She had a goal. Maybe it would have been useful to have her and the school working together for Darnell's sake."

"In the PTA?"

"Saturday meetings, bring in speakers from the police department, have the teachers explain curricula. I don't know. But, yes, in the PTA."

Heck shrugged, indifferent and resentful because of the uselessness of this discussion. "Might get a few more people to the meetings, but what's the point?"

"Parental involvement," Canaletti repeated as if he were instructing a young child.

"To me, that's a lot of time and work put in for very little gain."

"So how do you get your parents involved in the education of their children?"

"My teachers make phone calls to homes. I see people on the street in the neighborhood and I talk to them. I pass messages along through other parents. I see them at church."

"Those are slow and inefficient methods. How do parents

get general information about new initiatives in the school? How do they catch the fever of wanting to be part of changing trends? If people are together as a group, it helps to whip up feelings."

"Feelings for improved test scores?"

"Yes!"

"I guess they don't get that."

Canaletti sighed. "Right!" He looked at the other principals and gave up on Heck. "What about the rest of you? How can you beef up attendance in PTA at your schools?"

Heck consulted his watch. He had no reason to stay so he left, not caring what Canaletti might think. Instead of taking the elevator, he walked down the stairs, and he leaned against the railing. Now, he could hardly remember why he had walked out. But he felt guilty all of a sudden, like a student cutting class. So he pushed through the door and emerged on the second floor near Canaletti's office. He told the secretary that Canaletti had asked him to wait inside. It was that easy to get into the man's office.

He sat where he had sat before, facing Canaletti's desk. Wan light filtered through the venetian blinds, but otherwise the room was dark and stank of cigarette smoke. The desk was piled a foot deep with books, reports, files and articles.

Heck wondered how Canaletti would feel if this were swept to the floor, if the piles of papers on the filing cabinets were splattered with glass slivers and violated by filthy hands?

He got up and slowly circled the desk. He glanced at some of the memos and letters, interested to understand the questions and problems an associate superintendent faced.

Canaletti's chair was padded brown leather with brass tacks.

It swiveled, tilted back and rolled. If he had gotten the job, this would be his chair.

He lowered himself into it and placed his hands palms-down on the desk. He had worked in an office like this as a teenager. It had been a small, drafty room, overcrowded with desks, file cabinets and a worktable piled high with the records necessary to run an infinitesimally small part of the war. There had been dozens of such offices in the building where he had worked, in dozens of buildings hastily constructed on the mall not far from the Washington Monument.

It was an "advancement" that he was able to get the job. In 1941, President Roosevelt signed an executive order stating that there could be no discrimination in government-office or defense-plant hiring. Every living soul was needed to throw themselves into the war effort—even black souls.

So, in 1943, when he was sixteen, still in high school, he got a night job, alphabetizing cards, filing papers, collating, stuffing envelopes, stapling and sorting. That had been his first real job. And being principal at Grant would be his last. He understood that he would never rise any further than that.

Heck rubbed his eyes and tried to focus, but everything was blurry. He got up and felt dizzy. When he tried to walk, he fell against the file cabinets. He turned then, to see if he could read the lettering on the cabinets and was relieved that he could. A–C. H–J. J seemed like a cue. He opened the drawer and fingered through the files until he came to his own. The written record of his life, his personal history. He put the file under his arm, closed the drawer, and walked out.

The secretary was on the phone, writing a message. She waved at him as he left. But he had no energy to acknowledge her.

* * *

Heck heard Tina unlock and come in the front door. He heard the rustle of her coat as she took it off. He wanted to greet her, but somehow he couldn't even get his eyes open. He realized that he was sprawled out on the living-room floor. Vaguely he recalled feeling very weak and that the floor seemed as good a place as any to lie down.

"Daddy," Tina said quietly, then shrieked, "Daddy!"

He heard her, as if in the distance but he was too tired to move.

She grabbed his shoulders to rouse him, then tucked her head under his chin to listen for his heart. She was murmuring, "Daddy, Daddy, I'm sorry." And she was crying. Maybe she had been crying for awhile. He couldn't tell, but his shirt felt wet.

Why did his arms feel so leaden? Finally, he managed to raise an arm.

She screamed and jumped back. Her hair was all mashed on one side and her face was a ruin of tears and mascara. "Why didn't you say something? You scared me," she sobbed.

"I was asleep, I guess."

She scrambled to her feet and tried to rub the mess off her face. "What are you doing on the floor? I thought you were hurt or . . . That was a mean trick!"

He turned his head from side to side. He tried to chuckle. "Strange place for a nap."

"Why aren't you at school? It's four o'clock."

He tried to sit up, but the effort was too much. "Help me," he said. He raised his arms to her. She helped him to the sofa, and he slumped down next to the file folder he had taken from Canaletti's office. "It's been a weird day," he said.

"What's wrong with you?" she demanded.

He studied her smeared face. "What's wrong with *you*? A

second ago you were all over me, saying, 'Sorry.' Did you think I was dead?"

"Yes!"

"So now I'm alive again, you're back to being a terror?"

She didn't respond.

"What were you apologizing for?"

She threw out her arms. "If I'd ever hurt you. I don't know."

"Well, you do hurt me when you act like this."

"Like what?"

"Like you don't care about me or anyone else, not even about yourself."

"I care about people."

"Who?"

"None of your business."

"Oh, so this is all about a boy," he said, pulling himself erect on the couch.

"It's not that simple."

Heck squeezed the bridge of his nose. "For a minute there, I thought I had my lovable little Quintina back."

"Quintina." She snorted. "You don't care about me. All I ever was to you was the fifth one. You even named me Number Five. I'm supposed to tag along in the footsteps of my illustrious brothers and sisters. Graduate from Grant with honors, go to some highfalutin school like they did so you can say, 'Look, the school works. My own kids . . .' Well, I'm not there to glorify you, the almighty of mighty principals. I'm there for me. And I'll do as I please."

He groaned. "How did we get on to this?"

She pointed to the floor. "That was a dirty trick!"

"It wasn't a trick. It was a nap."

Eight huge gold hoops down the curve of one ear clacked

as she jerked her head around. "A nap? In the middle of the living-room floor in the middle of the afternoon?"

"Take out all those earrings."

"What?"

"I said you look like a fool. Take out the earrings."

"No." She pointed her finger at him. "See, that's just it. Black is wonderful. Only you don't really believe that. You have all this ambition—got to get ahead, move on top. Got to be the big administrator."

"What are you talking about? I've been at the same school for twenty-five years. But as a matter of fact, yes, I would have liked to move up. And what's wrong with that?"

She nodded as if she had won a point. "Oreo cookie. Black on the outside, white on the inside. You kissin' ass with Canaletti and any other person you can, shufflin' and grinnin' to get over your own upbringing, to move on up and be almost white. My sister's like that too. If she could bleach herself pure white, I bet she would so she'd fit in up there at Wellesley. I've talked to her. I know. An' you and Mom are the same. Always marching us around the neighborhood to be a great example to everyone. Want us to get on out of here, so we don't have to associate with our own neighbors and the kids at Grant. They ign'rant and lazy and dirty and po', and you hate 'em for that. But I don't. I have friends here. I like them. I feel sorry for all the stuff they have to put up with in their lives, not being so lucky as I am. And I won't betray them."

He stood up on shaky legs. "How did we get from earrings to betraying people? Nobody's asking you to betray anybody, only don't betray yourself, either. Let me tell you, those earrings are ugly!"

"See. You don't understand. And it doesn't seem like I can make you understand. But that's okay. I have places where I can go, to people I care about and who care about me, who think the same way. And you can't touch me there." She backed up. "Places where I'm loved for who I am." She marched across the room and out the door, leaving her books fanned out across the floor where she had dropped them when she had thought he was dead.

"I don't know what happened," Heck told Yvonne later. "I went into the man's office, unasked, when he wasn't there. I read his mail. I sat in his chair. I went into his file cabinet and stole my file. I violated his office. It's no different from what happened to me."

"I think we should go to the doctor, baby. This isn't right. That heart medicine, maybe it's gotten too weak," Yvonne said, holding his hand.

"I've been taking it for three years, since the surgery. It's never affected me before," he said.

"You've been under a lot of stress recently. You weren't yourself when you went into his office. You weren't in your right mind. Then to come home and fall asleep on the floor. Heck, you're sick, baby. Don't you see?"

"I'm going to take this thing back to him and apologize and tell him I'll retire at the end of this year."

"You don't need to retire. Just tell him you were sick."

"If I tell him I'm sick, he'll want me to resign immediately. I feel fine now, but I was talking all this nonsense at the meeting this morning. About Charlemagne." He put his hand over his eyes.

"I'll make a doctor's appointment first thing in the morning," Yvonne said.

"When Tina came in here she thought I was dead."

Yvonne threw her arms around him. "Baby, baby."

"It was a very deep sleep." He struggled to recall it. "I don't know why I lay down on the floor in the first place. Seemed like I could hardly move my arms at first when I woke up. My head was hurting so much. And I scared Tina. You know, I think she *wants* me dead."

"That child! I'm gonna tan her hide. She just ran out and left you?"

"She hates us, or me anyway."

"She doesn't. You know Tina. She's been walking through life with her hand on her hip and her mouth open."

"She's talking about leaving home."

"Lord, I say let her go. Then she'll see how nice she has it here."

"I'm afraid she might not come home *tonight*."

Yvonne rested her head on Heck's shoulder. She said quietly, "I hope she does."

"Me too."

They fixed dinner and ate without Tina. "I'm going to make up a plate for her that she can pop in the microwave when she gets here," Yvonne said.

"She won't eat it anyway. She'll just want ice cream," Heck predicted. "Causing us all this worry. It's not right."

"She's trying to make a point."

"Well, she's made it."

When the phone rang, they both jumped for it. Yvonne handed the receiver to Heck. "It's Danny. Don't stay on too long."

"Heck," Danny said. "Sorry to bother you."

"It's okay."

"Anya Cooper came to me today babbling something about Miz Brown. She was scared. You told her to come to me?"

"Right."

"Anyway, I had a little run-in with the lady. And Heck, I think she's got a gun in her desk drawer."

"What?" Heck wasn't sure he had heard her right. For a moment he thought the blurriness was coming back. He suddenly felt very warm.

"She said she wanted to kill Nick Tiebault she was so mad at him the other day. And she said she had the means, under lock and key in her desk drawer. She wears the key on her watchband."

He didn't want to believe her. "Danny, you know how you are about Miz Brown."

"It's crazy, I know. But she practically said, 'I've got a gun in here.' "

Heck tried to concentrate on what she was telling him. He heard the front door open.

"Okay. Okay, Danny. I hear you. I'll talk to you tomorrow," he said, watching Yvonne hurry out of the room.

He fell into a kitchen chair. He couldn't handle any more problems today.

Yvonne came back in with her arm around Tina's shoulders. "What's wrong now?" she said. "You look like a ton of bricks hit you."

"Mrs. Mitchell says she thinks Miz Brown has a gun in her desk."

"That couldn't be," Yvonne said.

"She said she was pretty sure."

Tina rolled her eyes in boredom, tapped her foot. This was because they weren't paying immediate attention to her, he supposed. Instantly, Heck was angry with her childish selfishness again.

"What are you doing here? I thought you had someplace you could go," Heck lashed out at her.

"I do. But he has to work tonight," Tina said defiantly. Yvonne damned Heck with a look. "Baby, I made you a plate of food," Yvonne said.

"I don't want any," Tina said. She spun out of Yvonne's grip and was gone. A moment later they heard her door upstairs slam.

Heck

HECK WAITED ON THE STAGE while classes and teachers filed into the auditorium. Parents and graduates were being ushered in another door for the annual Thanksgiving assembly. A yellow jacket, his walkie-talkie crackling, stood at one side of the stage. Another was stationed near the rear door to monitor the behavior of students filling the seats.

As he silently scanned the crowd, Heck could hear the nervous whispers of the choir lining up on the risers behind the moth-eaten stage curtain. He watched teachers handling their classes, noticing whether they ignored inappropriate behavior or swiftly dealt with it. He watched individual students for potential problems. He ticked off in his mind the names of various mothers and fathers and connected them with their children.

He thought it was important for the spirit and well-being of the school community to get everyone together. They needed to feel one another's presence, the power of their collectivity. They needed this group identity. And they needed to know that he felt confident of their maturity.

Today, in particular, when he would later be meeting with Canaletti to announce his retirement, he was glad an assembly had been planned. He needed to feel the warmth of the school family.

Thirty-six years ago, he'd started teaching. He'd been considered old to be a beginning teacher, but it had taken that long to put himself through school, and then there had been the two years in the service. On the other hand, he had brought wisdom to the job, he thought.

He leaned over the microphone and spoke calmly. "Take your seats." He gave them a few seconds, then repeated the command. "Take your seats now, please. Our program is about to begin."

He purposely spoke quietly so people would have to strain to listen. "Every year we come together on this day before the holiday. With family and graduated friends here, as well as with our present students, we can have some sense of ourselves as a community, of the ongoing history we are creating. Like any history, ours is complex and rich and bittersweet. We have much to still strive for. Much to be thankful for. As you listen to these songs, I'd like you to remember and think about what this school means and has meant to you, what the community has done for you. Now, I'd like to turn the program over to our music director, who has planned an enjoyable presentation for us."

Heck stepped off the stage as the curtains opened. There were hoots and whistles from the audience at seeing friends in their choir robes. Immediately, the choir launched into a gospel version of "Nearer My God to Thee." Some in the audience rose to their feet, to whoop and clap along as their teachers tried to settle them down.

Heck strode out into the foyer. It was traditional on this day for people to come and talk to him. Soon, a small group had gathered around him.

"I know you don't recognize this child," one mother said. She had her arm around the waist of a young man who towered over her. "I'm Mrs. Hardy and this is Terence."

Heck remembered Terence as a gangly kid, painfully shy. "What have you been eating, son?" he asked.

Mrs. Hardy was so proud, her smile looked like it might split her face. "I swear to goodness, he ain't stopped growing yet. And he's steady working."

"Where you working, Terence?"

"Children's Hospital . . . nights . . ."

Heck took his hand and shook it. "That's very fine. I appreciate you coming by. Where were you for our basketball team that year, huh?"

Mother and son both laughed, and Heck moved on.

"Dr. Jasper, you don't remember me," a panting, heavyset woman said. "My daughter was only here for a few months las' year in tenth grade till she got pregnant. That chile died, and my daughter, LaTicia, have never been the same since. She jus' mope aroun' the house, can't do nothin', talkin' about she jus' wanna die, be with that baby. You said a few words to her when she lef'. 'Come on back. We be waitin' for you.' Somethin' like that. I think she might make it on back here, if she thought that was really true. I tole her I'd come talk to you."

Heck took her elbow and steered her down the hall. "We would love to have her back here. You tell her to come directly to me."

"Thank you, Doctor. She jus' been so pitiful. She scarin' me to death."

"Send LaTicia in on Monday."

"I will."

"Well, now, look at this, will you?" He shook the hand of a young Marine in dress uniform.

"Home on leave, sir."

He touched the braid on the Marine's shoulder. "Looking mighty fine, too, Corporal Phillips. How'd you ever get them to take the likes of you?"

"I guess I had to gloss over a little bit of the past, sir."

Heck threw an arm over Phillips's shoulders and strolled down the hallway. "I always figured you were sent to my office so often because you liked to see me."

Phillips grinned. "Didn't like it at the time, sir."

"How many times I suspend you?"

"I don't know."

"Neither do I. But it's a wonderful thing about life how we most always get another chance. I see you made some good choices."

"Yes sir. I'm glad I did, too."

"Um hum. I know what you're saying. I was in the army."

"You were?"

"Korea. Always thought I'd love it. But I've loved this a whole lot better—this school and good kids like you coming back to see me."

"You were a good principal, sir," Phillips told him.

Heck blushed. "I gotta go look in on these hoodlums in here."

He left school after the final bell to meet with Canaletti. He adjusted the briefcase in his hand—the briefcase that held his file, which he was returning to Canaletti—and limped down the steps. The sun was bright so he kept his eyes on the sidewalk while he walked toward his car. Soon he picked up a trail of blood on the concrete. At first, there were just a few large red-brown drops, then a stream, then drops again. He followed them as he mentally reviewed the possibilities: a nosebleed, a fistfight, a gunshot or a stab wound.

"This black community is sick at heart," Miz Brown often said. What could be done about that? What could a school family do? What else should he try? A block from the school the drops of blood continued across the street, but he stopped at the curb as if he'd come to the end of a dock. To go any farther would be pointless. As Canaletti had said in their first meeting, "You can't deal with the whole city. You can only deal with what's inside your building."

For so long he'd believed in the forward motion of history; things would tend to get better. But too many lives were limited by generation after generation of poverty, ignorance, bloodshed, hopelessness. They might as well be back in chains.

He stood at the curb, unable to leave. He couldn't help feeling there was something more he should know about this trail of blood.

A car stopped. The driver, the parent of a former student whose name Heck couldn't recall, leaned over. "Need a lift, Dr. Jasper?"

"No, thank you."

"You feeling all right sir? You look all wore out."

Heck transferred the briefcase to his other hand and looked at his watch. He was going to be late if he didn't hurry. The gentleman's name popped into his head. "I *have* been feeling tired lately, Mr. Peebles. Never thought I'd slow down when I got older, but here I am at a complete stop."

Mr. Peebles chuckled. "I know 'bout that, too. If you on your way somewhere, I'd be glad to carry you there."

"On my way to my car," Heck pointed it out half a block back. "And I got to thinking about something else. How are Freddy and Martine doin'?"

"You got a remarkable memory, Doc."

"I remember all the real bad ones," Heck teased.

"Freddy works on the line for the phone company. Got three kids. Martine went to UDC for awhile. Now she's doin' computer work. And she sings with a band on the weekends."

"They were good kids."

"Thank you, sir."

"I gotta go."

"Uh huh. Catch you next time."

Heck turned around, retraced his steps, following the blood. He was going to be late unless he lucked out on the traffic. How could he have gotten so distracted, standing there at the curb like a fool? Yvonne had made him a doctor's appointment for the first thing next week, and he was looking forward to going. Maybe she was right, maybe something was wrong with his heart medicine. It was making his blood too thin, weakening him, making him light-headed and foolish.

He watched the red drops at his feet, each a pulse beat apart. He was on his way to tell Canaletti he was retiring, leaving this place that he'd given his heart and blood to for so many years. It wasn't a great achievement. It didn't merit a mention in the history books. It wasn't a monument with his name on it. But pride came from knowing he had given this school and this neighborhood the best he had to offer.

Canaletti's secretary told him to go right in.

"I got the message you wanted to see me," Canaletti said. "What can I do for you, Dr. Jasper?"

"I'd like to retire after this school year." It was easy to say, and he felt relieved. It was the right decision.

Canaletti stubbed out his cigarette.

"I guess that'll leave you free to hire someone to get you the results you need."

"I thought you were enjoying being the opposition voice in this district."

"Well, I was." Heck fingered the edges of the file. "The truth is, though, I'm not up to par physically. And I've done some pretty strange things lately that worry me. I think it's best if—"

"Like what?"

"Well." Heck slid the file onto Canaletti's cluttered desk. "Monday when I left the meeting early, I came down here, meaning to talk to you. I don't know exactly what happened, except that I blanked out and before I knew it, I was out the door with this file in my hands."

Canaletti picked up the file, read the name, and put it down again.

"The worrisome part is, I don't know why," Heck went on. "I have a doctor's appointment next week. Maybe it's my heart medicine." He shook his head. "I don't know. But I don't want to do something stupid at school."

"Carolingian minuscule?"

"Yes, that too. I don't know where that came from."

"You were giving me a pretty hard time in that meeting."

"Yes, sir." Heck half expected Canaletti to suggest he resign now. How could someone who'd committed these offenses expect to keep his job?

"You should have stayed in the meeting," Canaletti said.

"Yes, I should have."

"Because, as it turned out, after you left, quite a few of the other principals started agreeing with you that I was on the wrong track. I've been wondering about something. Do you think it's wrong to have a white man running a predominantly black system?"

The question caught Heck off guard. "Things have always been strange in America when it comes to race. We're supposed to work together."

"Yes. And the theory is that black and white can work together if we're all educated, sensitive and color-blind."

"No such thing as color blindness."

"Mutual respect, then. Colleagues trying to get a job done."

Heck raised his eyebrows. "Depends on the people."

"Am I the wrong person?"

"Why are you asking?"

"Because I've been asking myself this. When thirty or forty percent of my principals say I'm dodging issues, that I'm pursuing the wrong goals, then I've got to think about that. You've been challenging me all along and now you're leaving. I'd rather get to explore these questions than have you walk out the door. You're a very influential person in this system. People respect you. Maybe I could get you to work for me as a consultant. I wouldn't want people to think I've forced you out."

It was a little surprising to hear Canaletti talk like this. Heck had thought the man incapable of seeing beyond himself and his own close-minded ideas. But it was too late as far as Heck was concerned. "I'm not leaving because of you. I'm not trying to make a statement about you, and you can tell people that. I'm leaving because I'm tired. As you said, people bust up my office, it doesn't look good. Things are way out of control and I can't do anything about them. We need a strong leader in this office. You're not much better or worse than most of the other people, white or black, who've been in here."

Canaletti pulled on a cigarette. "Why do I feel so relieved? You tell me I'm doing a half-shitty job, and I feel relieved."

"'Cause it's not all shitty. *And* it's a lousy position you're in, to tell you the truth."

"Coming from you, Dr. Jasper, this sounds like a compliment."

"I wanted this job. Before you got it, I thought I should be the one to sit in that chair. I have enough rank. I know the district. I've put in a lot of time here."

"I figured you felt that way. I can understand that."

"Truth is, I wouldn't have liked it," Heck admitted. "Maybe I deserved it, but I wouldn't have been happy here. I like seeing kids' faces."

"Know why I took it?"

"No, why?"

"Any job I take bores me after a few years. I applied for this almost on a lark. I knew school systems have been experimenting with using business people. I wanted to see what I could do. It's been an experience."

"Are you bored yet?"

"Not bored. Not thrilled, either. I've had the experience twice of coming into a faltering company and turning it around and making it damned profitable. I thought I could do that here, too. A fine challenge. *And* if I could make it work, there would be the bonus of knowing I'd done something worthwhile, besides just making money."

"I'm glad to hear that."

"I'm not as hard-hearted as you think, Dr. Jasper. I started out as a teacher too. I care about education and about the young. I'm trying to make it work for them. But, it's not as easy as I thought."

He scooped up a sheaf of papers from his desk. "I've just been working on a set of proposals for some school-based community programs. An after-school nutrition and health program, a Saturday sports program, parent-teen drug treatment network. Maybe you'd like to look them over and give me your comments."

Heck couldn't work up any enthusiasm for Canaletti's agendas. He bounced from one enthusiasm to the next like a teenager himself. Heck felt a certain vindication, and he was glad Canaletti was proposing these things. But he wondered how far off his desk they'd actually get. He shook his head. "Everybody's seen a lot of *programs*. Programs don't solve problems. People do. People caring about people." Heck pointed to the papers. "In all those ideas, don't forget the people, even the littlest ones."

"Okay." Canaletti sighed and looked away. "You know, when you left the meeting on Monday, I said, 'What *was* he talking about? Carolingian minuscule?' I was meaning to discredit you. Mrs. Pepper said, 'I don't know what he meant by that, but Hector Jasper *always* knows what he's talking about.' And that's when everyone began discussing your ideas and your school. You're a good teacher, Dr. Jasper. A thorn in the side, but a good one."

Heck shrugged. He couldn't even remember what he'd said that day besides the inappropriate reference.

"The funny part is," Canaletti went on, "that night I got to thinking over the meeting and the Charlemagne reference struck an odd chord in me. I came from a religious family. Lots of kids. My mother named all the boys after popes. I'm Leo. It was Leo the Third who crowned Charlemagne."

Heck didn't know whether he or Canaletti was the strange one. What was Canaletti talking about?

"Charlemagne did more to improve the lot of people in medieval times than any papal leader. He was effective and devout. It struck me how little I understand about the needs of this system and the people in it and how much you know."

"The general in the field always knows more than the one at the desk," Heck said, wishing he could be spared Canaletti's seemingly aimless talk.

"Yes. But the story goes that they needed each other. Leo needed Charlemagne to consolidate the empire within the church's realm—to unite the Holy Roman Empire. And Charlemagne wanted Leo to crown him emperor. Charlemagne wanted to be recognized for all he'd done, recognized even by God—or at least God's emissary on earth."

"What are you getting at?" Heck asked, confused by Canaletti's philosophizing.

"I don't know. Why did you bring up Charlemagne?"

"I was drifting."

"Pope Leo, of course, was totally overshadowed by Charlemagne. He took orders from him after the coronation."

Heck was feeling the pressure behind his eyes again. He couldn't follow the turns in the conversation or the implications. Canaletti intended the story to have underlying meaning. But Heck's vision was getting blurry again, and he concentrated on that because it scared him now. He wondered if he'd be able to drive home.

"There can really only be one leader in any system," Canaletti said, "if the system is to work effectively for the people. That was the lesson I came away with."

He held out his hand. "Have a good Thanksgiving, Dr. Jasper. Rest. Take it easy. It's going to be very hard to replace you. But, I think it's for the best, between the two of us."

Cirri

SICK AS SHE WAS, MAMA WAS
gone when Cirri brought the kids home from the bus stop on
Wednesday. The kids didn't think anything of it, of course.
That was Mama's usual routine. They were excited because
they'd had holiday assemblies in school. There was a Swahili
word, *chakula*, that Willie kept saying over and over about
food and the harvest. They found the kitten and started dragging a string for it to chase.

But Cirri was worried. The brown bottle of medicine was
sitting unopened in the middle of the kitchen table. How
could Mama have gone out? She was too sick. Did she mean
to stay out all night? It was too cold. She had that debt to pay,
though. How was she going to pay it? Cirri didn't want to
think about it.

She sat down at the table and held her head in her hands.
There was no food in the house. Marcus was off somewhere

with Tina. Maybe he was taking her to Mimi's house right now. Mama was gone. Furry was long gone. Who was left? Thea had said to come on over for Thanksgiving dinner, but that was tomorrow, hours away. What would she do between now and then? She had no one.

The kids were squealing in the other room. How could they be having a good time? "Shut up!" she yelled at them. "Too much damn noise."

Hungry, she got up, opened the refrigerator and found only a loaf of bread, a dab of margarine, a little jelly, an empty carton of milk. She slammed the door and leaned against it. At school they had been collecting canned food for the needy and homeless. She remembered the homemade signs and the PA announcements. Would she qualify as needy? Soon enough, she thought, her own family would be homeless. People were evicted even out of this ugly old building. She had seen furniture and belongings downstairs on the curb more than once. Someone would be standing over the things, keeping the neighbors from taking what they wanted.

For three months now, there had come a notice in the mail that she'd opened and thrown away. *Pay the rent*, it said. *You owe this much*. Last time it had been close to a thousand dollars. Where was she supposed to get money like that? Might as well be asking for ten thousand. She couldn't come up with that kind of money at McDonald's.

She slumped down at the table again. If she could just get some canned soup or peaches. She wondered whether school was still open. Even if she got there in time, would they give her any of the food?

Mrs. Mitchell would sneak Cirri a few cans if they hadn't already all been taken away. Mrs. Mitchell had tried to call once, Cirri remembered. She would help if she could. But it was four o'clock. More than likely, the school was locked up.

Her thoughts were interrupted by a whining at the front door. Was it another cat? She got up and listened with her ear to the door. When she finally opened it, she found Mama sprawled on the floor, her lip bleeding, her eye swollen, her hair full of blood. Cirri looked up and down the hallway, then pulled Mama into the apartment and slammed the door.

"Baby, I . . . baby, I . . ." Mama muttered, her body shaking.

Cirri sat her against the wall and ran for a washcloth. The kids crept up to her, but were too horrified to say anything. Cirri dabbed at the blood dribbling down Mama's chin and held the cloth against her head. "Willie, go get me another washcloth," she ordered. "Hurry!"

"Mama?" Pea wailed. "Whatsa matter, Mama?"

Mama grew rigid with a coughing fit, then slumped against Cirri. "Baby, I . . . baby . . ."

Willie returned with the cloth, which Cirri pressed against Mama's lip. She winced and yanked Cirri's hand away. Her head bobbing, she held out her arms. Pea lunged into Mama's embrace. "Come he-here, big ma-han," Mama said, and Willie edged in next to Pea. "I . . . I . . . I loves you," she whispered. "Loves you so . . . so much."

While she held the kids with one arm, she thrust out her other arm triumphantly toward Cirri. Clutched in her fist were salt and pepper shakers taken from McDonald's. "For s-supper," she told Cirri. Then she slid across the wall sideways and fell. Her head hit the doorjamb.

Pea screamed. Willie jumped back. "Is she dead?"

"No!" Cirri pulled Mama back up, hugged her and held Mama's cheek against her own. She needed to feel the warmth, the life. "But she gonna be if we don't get her to a doctor. I shoulda took her a long time ago. Get your coats. Come on."

With Mama stumbling between them, Cirri and Willie got

her down the stairs and outside. Occasionally, she lifted her head and appeared to realize that she was going somewhere. She'd manage to walk a few steps. Then her head would loll forward while they dragged her. Her whole body shook, though Cirri didn't know whether it was the sickness or because of the drugs.

They attracted a small crowd as they struggled with Mama across the broad stretch of concrete to the street. Pea was crying and hanging on to Cirri's coat. "What's wrong wid her, man?" asked a couple of the boys hanging out on the corner.

"She sick!"

"Where you takin' her?"

"To the doctor. Where you think?"

It was getting dark. Cirri could make out the hustlers in the shadows.

One man hurried up to them. "What happened?"

"Nothing. She just bad sick."

"Want me to drive her somewheres? My car's over there."

Cirri had no money for bus fare. She didn't even really know where she was going. But she didn't trust this guy. "No. My boyfriend's coming to get us," she said. "He gonna be here right now."

"Sure now?"

"Yeah."

Cirri watched him go while Mama, limp now, slid further down Cirri's side.

"Marcus coming?" Willie asked, hopeful. "He have a car?"

"No," Cirri whispered.

"When will Marcus get here?" Pea cried.

Cirri threw Mama's arms over her shoulders. Willie tried to carry Mama's legs. But it was awkward.

"I want Marcus," Pea whined.

"Be quiet!" Cirri scolded. "He's not comin'. That was just a story."

Finally, they got Mama to the curb and sat her down. Willie knelt behind her and held her. Cirri craned to see whether the man was gone, then she darted out into the street in the near darkness and waved her arms at the oncoming headlights.

At last a car stopped. A well-dressed couple helped them get Mama into the backseat. She had a coughing fit then and Cirri was afraid that the people might put them back out on the curb. But the man just said, "Which hospital?"

"Any one. The closest one that'll take us."

"That'll be the General."

The woman turned around in her seat and studied them. "We're Mr. and Mrs. Davis. Who're you?"

Cirri introduced the family.

"She do sound mighty sick. She been this way long?"

"Few days."

When they pulled up at the emergency room, the man turned off the motor and said, "Wait here."

"He's a paramedic," Mrs. Davis said. "He'll get some action for you."

Two ambulances were parked at the door. Their bright flashing lights hurt Cirri's eyes. Pea was whimpering. Willie sat in stunned silence. Mama was slumped between them, breathing loud and fast.

"Not a good way to start Thanksgiving," Mrs Davis said.

Mr. Davis returned, pushing a low bed on wheels. He opened the back door and helped Pea and Willie out. Then he reached in, gathered Mama up and swung her onto the bed. He covered her with a blanket, and buckled a strap across her. "Okay, we'll get her logged in."

Mr. Davis parked Mama's bed along a wall and went to talk to a nurse at the desk. Cirri stayed with Mama, but she watched Mr. Davis gesture toward Mama and toward Pea and Willie who were sitting with Mrs. Davis in the waiting area.

Mrs. Davis came up to Cirri and took her hand. "You probably gonna be here awhile. This place is always busy. Take this money and go on down the cafeteria. Get them kids something to eat. Pea and Willie. Right?"

Cirri looked at the bill in her hand. It was a ten.

"Okay," Mr. Davis said, striding back to them. "They got a stabbing, a heart attack, a DOA coming, coupla fractures from a car wreck. But I got you top of the list after that 'less something else comes up more serious." He pulled up one of Mama's sleeves and studied the scars. "If she gets too restless, they'll give her something. You did the right thing to bring her in."

"Think they'll be anything to do with the police or anything like that?"

"No, they're just gonna try and get her well."

Cirri nodded.

"We gotta go," Mrs. Davis said.

"Okay." Cirri was remembering what Mama had said about the police. She'd been wrong. They should have gone to a clinic a long time ago.

The Davises were walking out the door. Cirri ran to them. "Hey! Thanks!" she shouted.

Around ten o'clock, the doctor came to talk to Cirri. "Are you the next of kin?"

"Yes."

"Is there an adult? Husband? Parents?"

"No."

He sat down across from the kids. Pea was asleep. Willie was watching the TV. "Your mother has pneumonia in both lungs," he told Cirri quietly. "She's dehydrated and malnour-

ished. She got beaten up tonight. We stitched up her scalp."
He paused. "She's real sick. She'll have to stay here awhile."

Cirri didn't take her eyes off him. She wanted to get every
word he was saying, but the seriousness of what he said scared
her, made her mind skip to other things. There were two gray
hairs in his sideburn. One lens of his glasses was chipped.

"Do you and your brother and sister have someplace to stay
while she's here?" he asked.

"Yes."

"Okay. If she responds to the medicine, maybe she can go
home in three or four days, but even then she'll still be weak."

Cirri nodded.

"She'll have to eat well and take care of herself in order to
really shake this. Can you manage that?"

"Yes."

"You know she has a chemical dependency, don't you?"

"What?"

"She has an addiction."

Cirri wasn't sure what she should reveal. "I guess so."

"She won't ever get well unless she gets help for that. We're
going to talk to her about it while she's here. We've got a
place we can send her once she's over the pneumonia."

"Send her where?"

"A treatment facility. But you kids have to have a place to
stay. Is there an adult who'll take you in? We've got to know
that."

"I want to see her," Cirri said.

"She's being processed. Just exactly where are you staying
tonight?"

Cirri panicked. What had she done? She'd turned Mama in.
And now this doctor was going to take her and the kids away
from Mama just like Mama had said.

She quickly thought up a story. "We live with my gran'-

mother! You want the address? She had to stay home with the twins. Otherwise she'd be here. We weren't going to bring those babies out on a night like this." She stood up. "Now I want to see my mother."

He seemed to accept her lie. "You can see her in a little while, as soon as she's settled in her room. But they're getting the IVs in now, cleaning her up, trying to get some fluids down her."

"Where is she?" She had to get Mama out of here as soon as possible.

"She's fine, I promise you. Nothing is going to happen to her. In a couple of days she'll be better. But those little kids can't go up and see her. It's not allowed. And I wouldn't leave them here alone. The best thing you can do is go home to your grandmother and put them to bed and get some sleep yourself."

She was tired. Her eyes stung. Mama *did* need to be here; she knew that. She had pneumonia. Let them get her feeling better. Then Cirri would put up a fuss, if she needed to, to get Mama out. She scowled at him as a warning. If anything happened to Mama, if they tried to put her someplace or turn her in, he was going to get those glasses smashed right into his eyes. She went back, picked up Pea, shook Willie, and trudged out the door.

She had four dollars left from the ten. It hadn't seemed like too long of a ride to get here. She headed toward the front of the hospital to get a cab.

Tina Jasper was coming out of the front door with her mother. They were buttoning their coats and walking fast with their heads down. The first thought that came to Cirri was that Marcus had been hurt. Mr. Davis had mentioned a stabbing. She imagined Marcus's blood, like Mama's, running down his face.

Carrying Pea, Cirri hurried to intercept Tina. "Why you here?" she demanded. "Is it Marcus?"

Tina scowled at her. "Marcus? No. My father's in there."

"Your father?" Cirri had been so convinced that it was Marcus that it didn't immediately register who Tina's father was.

Mrs. Jasper spoke. "Dr. Jasper's taken ill. Are you a student at Grant?"

Cirri nodded. She'd seen Mrs. Jasper at school once or twice. Now it all fell together.

"You'll hear about it on Monday," Mrs. Jasper said. "He's going to be all right."

Then they walked on, heading for the parking lot.

A cab pulled up and Cirri, Willie and Pea got in. Cirri held Pea on her lap so she could sleep better. Cirri rested her head on Pea's head and worried about all that she needed to do the next day.

Danny

DANNY WAS GLAD WHEN GUY called to remind her about their date on Wednesday. He seemed to take on charm the longer she was away from him. She remembered his planning the picnic, bringing a beer for her, how relaxed she felt. Rolls was set to spend the night at a friend's house. She could stay out late Wednesday without guilt and sleep in the next morning. The idea of having a civilized dinner in a restaurant took on grand proportions as the day wound down.

None of the students could be prompted to do much of anything on the days before holidays. She had made crossword puzzles of their vocabulary words for them, and they spent some time doing those. But most of the time she spent talking with them informally about their plans for the holiday, music, street etiquette, their neighborhood. It wasn't time wasted.

More and more kids left school as the day went on, so that by last period no one reported to her class. She locked the door and went to her office, where Miz Brown found her a few minutes later.

Miz Brown closed the door. She looked enraged. "Where is it?" she demanded.

"Where's what?"

"You know what, you meddling bitch."

Danny stood up. "You can turn right around and leave if that's the way you're going to speak to me."

"I should have known you couldn't be trusted. Me and my big mouth. You strut around here like you own half the school."

"What are you talking about?"

Miz Brown lifted the key on her watchband. "It's gone. You jimmied my desk. Now give it to me. It's registered in my name."

Danny narrowed her eyes. "So it *was* a gun."

"Don't play dumb with me. Give it to me."

This would mean Miz Brown's job, at least. But had Heck jimmied her desk? No, he would have told her to get rid of the gun, and because he liked her, he would have pretended the gun had never been there. "I'm going to tell you something scary, Miz Brown," she said.

"What?"

"I don't have it."

"No one else knew it was there."

"You threatened Nick with it. Who else did you threaten? Who else did you brag to about what you had in your drawer? The kids aren't dumb. Don't you think they could figure out what you meant by tapping your fingernails on that locked drawer? You meant them to get the point. And they did."

Her eyes were squinted with rage. "Give it to me."

"It's not here. Some kid's got it."

"How could they get in? I always keep my room locked when I'm not there."

"I'd say it's going to be interesting when someone gets shot and the police find out the gun's registered in your name. Are you going to report it missing?" Danny was enjoying seeing Miz Brown's discomfort.

"Of course not."

"Then it's going to be ticklish for you. What if some kid's thinking about threatening you with it?"

"That was the first thing I thought of."

"Why was that the first thing, I wonder?"

"Because these are very violent children!" Miz Brown rushed out and slammed the door.

Danny felt vindicated. But why hadn't Heck done something? That troubled her, for Heck's sake.

Later, before Guy came, she called Heck's house. Yvonne answered. There was a high note of fear in her voice. Heck had been admitted to the hospital. The doctor thought he was having mini-strokes. His blood pressure was high. He was resting, and the doctor said he could probably come home tomorrow for Thanksgiving. But it had been an awful afternoon. In fact, the last several days had been awful. She didn't know when he'd be back at school.

So that explained why he hadn't done anything about Miz Brown, Danny thought. Then she called a florist and had a bouquet sent to him.

She half wanted Guy to drive her to the hospital. She was worried about Heck. But the tone of Yvonne's voice made her consider. The family had had a scare. They needed private

time and space to collect themselves. Instead, she poured out
the whole story as Guy drove to the restaurant.

When they pulled into the parking garage, she realized she
didn't even know where they were. Guy got out and came
around to her side, to open the door for her.

"I'm sorry. I didn't realize how much I was going on. I'll
stop now. I promise," she said.

"You don't have to. I like hearing you talk."

"You do?"

"Yeah. You care about your job. That's different."

"Different from who?"

"Don't start that. Different from most people. Okay?"

"Where are we going?"

"Little expensive Italian place around the corner."

She smiled at his bluntness. "Expensive?"

"It's probably not any better'n Smokin' Ray's Ribs, which
was where I thought we'd go. But I figured you'd like this
more."

He held her hand as they emerged from the garage onto the
sidewalk. All of a sudden, she felt wonderful. There were
Christmas displays in the shops, tiny white sparkling lights on
bare branches, a holiday spirit. The air was brisk; her hand
was warm in his. He wore his cowboy boots and the heels
rang out on the sidewalk.

She studied his face as they walked. His looks, as always, excited her. "You're all dressed up."

"Sure. Every now and then I like to get the hair in my nose
trimmed."

She laughed.

They stopped. He was looking at her, smiling. "Feels good,
don't it?"

She wasn't sure if he was referring to getting dressed up, the laughter, or the whole evening. But she had to agree. It did feel good.

He put his arm around her and squired her through the restaurant door.

"I just look at the education Rolls is getting compared to what the kids at Grant are getting and it's clear that those kids are never going to compete. And that's in every school in the city." The drinks before and the wine with dinner had loosened her up. She was back on her favorite subject. "They can read, they can write sentences, sort of. And *when* they come to school, they can learn.

"But they're so far behind it's hard to think they can ever catch up. In eighth grade, Rolls is doing work my eleventh- and twelfth-graders can't do—long, complicated research papers. At Grant, they go to the library and copy things from the encyclopedia and most teachers accept that. They accept everyone copying off each other. Teachers know it's not right, but they've lowered their standards so much, they're just happy if a kid turns something in. It meant that he spent *some* time in front of an open book or, at least, copying complete sentences. The teachers think maybe some of it will sink in."

She tore off a piece of bread and used it to soak up the marinara sauce.

"If some teachers fight to maintain standards, it means they're giving out mostly D's and F's. The average grade point average at that school is one point four. D-plus. Some teachers give pep talks. 'Let's try for C's this advisory period.' Even when the honor-roll students do get A's and B's, the grades don't mean the same thing as A's and B's in the suburbs. We give a grade sometimes just to encourage a kid. So, okay, he didn't quite do the work up to par, but let me give him the B this time, pat him on the back, bring him along. Show him he can do the work, maybe he'll earn the grade next time. So let's say he does earn the B or A next time. He feels good, thinks he's the greatest. But put him up against some white kid out in the suburbs who got a B, and it wouldn't mean the same thing at all. Those kids are learning a lot more. They're going to be better prepared for everything—tests, college, jobs, life."

Her cheeks were hot. She knew she was stuck like a needle in a groove, but she had to finish. His face was soft in the candlelight. He looked interested, but she didn't really care if he was or not. She was too wound up to stop.

"But the worst part of all is that the kids don't know that they're getting screwed. They write essays about how they can be anything they want to be and about how smart they are and that there is a place for them in the world. It's all the civil-rights and black-pride rhetoric. Black history, Afro-centric studies: 'Look at all these amazing black men and women. They did it. You can too.' Rolls doesn't get all that stuff. He gets a taste of black-history during black-history month, but meanwhile, he's studying all the other people, all the other history, the concepts, the patterns, the techniques in science and English and math. The time spent on those things is what is going to stand him in good stead when it comes to SATs. The kids at Grant have plenty of confidence, but no competence. They're failing now and they don't even know it. They're doing low-level work and they'll continue to do the low-level work all their lives, as unskilled laborers, janitors, security guards, file clerks, couriers. After some efforts to make it in college, after a couple of pregnancies, after their confidence is all beaten out of them, they'll be glad to take shit work. And we'll be glad they're doing it. It's the American way. A perpetual class system based on race." She downed the rest of her wine. "A free and compulsory education. That's what we provide in this country. But the system is never equal. So we're teaching class. 'Stay in your class.' "

"Why don't you get a job in the suburbs?" he asked.

"Those kids are gonna make it. No matter what. The kids at Grant . . . I don't know."

"A crusader."

" 'A flaming asshole liberal' were my ex-husband's exact words."

"He didn't think the same as you."

She chuckled. "No."

"Did you love him?"

She was light-headed from the wine and her nonstop oratory. "Sure, for a while. Longer than he loved me, I think. Did you love Cheryl?"

"Right up to the time she divorced me."

Danny understood all at once. "So you still do love her. Except you're mad at her."

"I wouldn't say that."

"See, by the end, with Royce and me, it was mutual hate. But you and Cheryl. I mean, if she wants you back . . ."

"Cheryl's not all I thought she was."

"What's that supposed to mean? Nobody's perfect."

He reached for his wallet. "And especially *she's* not perfect."

"How 'bout we split this?"

"Why?"

"I've been employed all this fall."

"Bullshit." He signaled to the waiter for the check. "Do you want some dessert?"

"I couldn't eat another bite."

They commented on lights and decorations as they drove to her house. She had slid halfway across the seat and he had pulled her over to him. But the gear shift was in the way of her legs, so she had to sit sideways and recline against his shoulder. Her excitement rose. At one red light, they kissed until the cars behind them started honking.

At her house, he turned off the engine. With both hands free, he gathered her against him. She'd been hungry for this for a long time. Her skin hurt with sweet panic. "Come inside," she whispered.

He followed her silently.

He was sensitive. She'd forgotten how powerful and sweet it could be. She'd forgotten how significant it could seem. They held each other for a long time afterward, not wanting to let go.

Guy rolled onto his back. "Whatever happened with Jasper's office?"

"It was probably a kid named T-man."

"I'm a weak person," he said. "I wanted that job."

"What you did was poor judgment. That's not necessarily weakness."

"I feel like there's always a side of me that I can't trust. One side says, 'Hey, that's wrong. You can't do that.' The other side says, 'Lighten up. You gotta take things to the limit.'"

He took a deep breath. "When the cops were grilling me, they supplied all the details. 'Made the key from a wax impression, didn't you? Brought in one of the girls and raped her, then shattered all the glass to show her you meant business, that she better not squeal. Get back at all the authorities you've ever hated in your life. Right? Isn't that it, Tomblin?'"

"You didn't wreck the office, Guy," Danny said.

He faced her. "I've thought about it a lot. Their explanations fit. It could've been me."

"Did you want to rape any of those girls?"

"Thought went through my mind."

She stared straight up. "I don't believe you."

"That's what I'm saying. Could've been me."

"What are you saying? Was it you or not?"

"I'm saying I'm messed up."

She leaned up on one elbow. "Are you saying I've just made love to a rapist?"

He chuckled. "Didn't seem like a rape."

"Will you just give me straight answers?"

"I've never raped anybody. I didn't do Jasper's office."

"Okay."

"Make you feel better?"

"Yeah. I guess."

"See what I mean? If you've already been guilty of the temptation and someone says you actually did do it, your mind can work on you. Mine can."

"You've got an overly active conscience."

"Maybe."

She ran both hands up through her hair, impatient and frustrated with his talk.

"You just don't know me at all," he murmured.

She felt him watching her. It bothered her that she didn't know what he was thinking, but at the same time, she didn't want him to say another word.

In the middle of the night, she heard him getting dressed. "What's going on?" she mumbled.

"I think I better go."

"Rolls won't be home till ten or so."

"It's not Rolls."

"What then?"

"It's me. I like to sleep in my own bed."

She tried to wake herself up. "Jesus."

He bent over and kissed her, holding his boots in one hand.

"Sorry." Then he tiptoed down the stairs and put on his boots at the front door. She heard the heels ringing out on the sidewalk as he walked to the truck. Heard the engine roar, fade away.

She rolled over and tried to get warm again and fall back to sleep, but she couldn't. He was going back to Cheryl. And maybe, she thought, that was just as well.

Cirri

CIRRI REMEMBERED WAKING UP
with Marcus next to her. She remembered being warm then.
She turned over and dragged the thin blanket with her. Now
it was Tina who was warm. Cirri had never seen Tina being
friendly or sweet. Could she care for Marcus the way Cirri
did? Didn't Marcus notice the difference? Cirri remembered
Tina's scowl last night. What if it *had* been Marcus who was
in the hospital? Would Tina have cared?

She forced herself out of bed and went to make butter-and-
jelly sandwiches from the remaining bread. She cut them in
quarters, arranging them in a circle on a plate. She set two
glasses of water next to the plate in the center of the table.
Then she woke up Willie. She made him sit up so he would
remember her instructions. "I'm going to see Mama."

"I wanna go," he whined.

"Ssh. Don't wake up Pea. You can't go. They don't allow

little kids in. 'Sides, I haven't got the bus fare for you two. I made you some breakfast. When Pea wakes up, you two watch cartoons. And I'll be back soon as I can."

He looked like he was about to cry. She remembered how good he'd been yesterday, helping her with Mama, not complaining and whining like Pea, just doing what had to be done.

"Know what we're doing this afternoon?"

"What?" he said glumly.

"Going to Thanksgiving dinner. All you can eat."

"Where?"

"Thea's. And you can tell 'em your Swahili *chakula* chant, all about the harvest. They'll like that."

He slid back down onto his pillow and smiled at her, satisfied.

She stood up. "Don't let nobody in that door. An' be nice to your sister."

It was raining, so she pulled her coat collar up around her neck. Her hair was going to be a mess at Thea's, but there was no helping that. The streets were practically empty. She knew it would be a long wait for the bus, so she stood in a doorway near the stop and hunched her shoulders against the damp. There was trash in the gutter. It had dammed up the rainwater into a filthy pool. She watched the rings spread when the drops hit the surface and hoped Mama would be better this morning so she could tell her not to worry, that the police wouldn't bother her. Everyone just wanted her to get well. Because, now, in the daylight, with her head clearer, the doctor didn't seem too bad. He wanted to get Mama straight. He wanted to make sure that Cirri and the kids would be okay. He was like those other people, the couple in the car. He was helping out.

She stamped her feet to keep them warm and peeked out to look for the bus. Holiday schedule.

She was freezing by the time she got to the emergency room. There were quite a few people there already. She hoped she wouldn't have to wait.

"Dr. Brunson's not here. Why do you need to see him?" the receptionist said when she asked for the doctor.

"He put my mother somewhere in the hospital and I don't know where."

"Ask at Patient Information. Go back outside and around the front."

She plunged back out into the rain and hurried around the block of buildings to where she'd waited for the taxi last night.

At Patient Information they had no record of a Ruby James. Cirri felt the fear start to rise.

"When was she admitted?"

"Last night."

" 'Bout what time?"

"Nine or ten."

"Okay, then. She's going to be on a different list. Just a minute." The information lady made a phone call. "Room six-oh-six," she said finally. "Sixth floor."

She found Mama's room and tiptoed in. But Mama wasn't in any of the four beds, all of which had been slept in.

A toilet flushed behind a closed door nearby. Then the door swung open, and Cirri waited for Mama to come out.

A nurse backed out first, maneuvering a pole on wheels, but the woman connected by tubes to the pole wasn't Mama. Cirri figured Mama was getting this sort of attention too. Maybe there was another bathroom.

"Can I help you?" the nurse asked.

"I'm looking for my mother, Ruby James."

"She done walked outta here seven o'clock dis mornin'," said one of the other patients. "I tole the nurses. She done jus' got up, pulled out her IV, took her coat and walked out."

"We went looking for her," the nurse said to Cirri. "But she slipped out."

"She was a junkie," the other woman said. "Dat's what dey do. I been in here lotsa times wid dis diabetes, an' I seen it befo'."

The nurse nodded. "She's right. They don't generally stay."

"Dat's a junkie for you," the other woman went on. "No tellin' what dey'll do. Don't care 'bout a hang."

Cirri walked out and backtracked to the nurse's station. "Where's my mother?" she demanded. "Ruby James."

The nurse consulted her list, then looked up. "Left this morning on her own, against medical advice."

Cirri hit the counter, then swung away and headed for the elevator. It was all their fault. Didn't they realize how scared Mama was, how sick? And now she was out in that cold rain.

She had to find Mama. Dr. Brunson said she'd be sick and weak for a long time. Out in that cold, she'd die. She ran out the front door. Then she stopped, not knowing where to go.

Paralyzed, she watched the people come and go. They carried flowers and baskets of fruit under their umbrellas. They were going to visit patients who were grateful to be in clean, warm beds out of the rain, grateful for the medicine and the help they were getting.

And there, coming up the sidewalk under a red umbrella, was Tina Jasper. Cirri blocked her way.

"How's your father?" she asked.

"Fine. He's coming home this morning. What're you doing here again?"

"Don't you like to see me?"

"Not especially. Not with your attitude problem. Get out of my way."

"Why would I have an attitude problem?"

"I wouldn't know."

Tina tried to dodge, but Cirri blocked her. "Your mother in there with your father?"

"Get out my way, girl."

Cirri wouldn't let her pass. "Ain't that nice. You got your mama and your daddy and Marcus, too."

"What you talkin' about?"

"An' I got nobody," Cirri snarled. "Nobody!"

"What you talkin' 'bout Marcus? You're crazy."

Cirri felt for the key in her pocket. "Why should you have everybody and I have nobody? Marcus was mine, you slut. You don't care 'bout him." She raised her hand up with the key tucked in her palm. "But you had to have him. Didn't you?"

Tina backed up, looking scared. "Leave me alone."

"Admit it! You don't care about him," Cirri screamed. She charged at Tina and raked the key down her cheek.

Tina punched Cirri in the face, dropped the umbrella and felt her cheek. Cirri flew at Tina again and rammed her against a fence.

People gathered around them, yelling for them to stop.

Tina, her teeth bared, her cheek bleeding, ran back at Cirri. They grappled with each other, slugging and scratching until a couple of men finally pulled them apart.

Tina dabbed at the wounds on her face with her coat sleeve. "You bitch!" she shrieked. "No! Marcus ain't nothing to me! Nick is my man. Nick!"

Cirri wanted a hot bath. She thought about it all the way home. Something to stop the continuous shivers, something to soothe the bruises and scratches, something to calm the wild thoughts racing through her head. Mama was gone. Marcus had not left her for Tina. What should she do?

Because Tina was the one bleeding, people had helped her into the hospital. Cirri had wrenched herself free of the arms that restrained her. She had cursed at them so they'd stand back and leave her alone. Then she ran off into the rain. She kept running till she was well away from the hospital. She didn't want anyone coming after her. After a while, she had slowed and kept up a steady pace. The streets and sidewalks were empty.

When she unlocked the door to the apartment, she was suddenly scared. A grown man was sitting there watching cartoons with the kids. Then Pea shouted, "Furry's here! Furry's here!" and the man unfolded his legs and came to greet her.

"Willie tole me and tole me 'bout how he wasn't s'pose to let nobody in this place," Furry said. "Don't be too hard on him. I tole him I thought it'd be all right."

Cirri's throat hardened. Her eyes began to fill.

Furry touched her chin. "You look like you been in a fight."

She went into the kitchen and leaned against the refrigerator with her back to him.

He followed her along with Willie and Pea. "Look 'bout like a drowned dog, too. Where you been?" Furry asked.

"Where *you* been?" Cirri demanded. She didn't want him to see her cry.

"Lorton." He paused. "Then I came home to fine out a cat been named after me. A cat!"

Pea giggled.

"It's 'cause we like you," Willie said earnestly.

"I know you do. An' I 'preciates it. Just, I never had a namesake before. It takes some getting used to."

"We were scared. We didn't know what happened to you," Cirri said, angry.

"Well, I got burned out. Lived out on the street awhile till I got picked up. That's all. I shoulda wrote."

Cirri opened the refrigerator like she was busy, too busy to listen to all this.

"Kids say your mama's in the hospital. Willie say it's pneumonia."

"Willie knows a lot."

"She feeling better this morning?"

"Up walking around," Cirri said.

"When we going to Thea's?" Willie asked.

"Look at you in them clothes. Wore 'em for three days now. You going like that? Go get some clothes on."

"Can I wear my pretty dress?" Pea asked.

"It's too little for you and it's too cold outside."

"No, it ain't."

"Go on!"

Furry watched the kids leave the room. Then he sat down at the table.

Cirri gingerly put her hand to her aching cheek.

"A Thanksgivin' Day fight," Furry said. "First thing in the mornin', too. Uhn, uhn, uhn. You changed since I been gone!"

"How?"

"Used to be you was as sweet an' innocent as them kids. Cute as can be."

"Uh huh. Well, I guess if I didn't have to deal with people putting junk in their bodies and looking over their shoulders for the hustlers and the police after them, I could still be all innocent and such."

"It's good your Mama's gettin' help. I got some help at Lorton."

"She's not gettin' help. She walked out the hospital this morning before I even got there. She out in all that rain someplace, sick to death with pneumonia and needing her goddamned fix."

Furry put a hand across his eyes. "Dear Jesus."

"An' we ain't got no money, no food. Nothin'!" Cirri put her hands on her hips. "You an' all the junkies workin' hard to kill yourselves and leave behind all these sweet little kids. What we s'posed to do, huh? How we s'posed to handle that?"

"I could find her, maybe," he mumbled.

That was the first reasonable thing he'd said. Cirri softened. "Do you think so?"

"I could try. I used to know some a' her spots."

Cirri sighed. "I don't know where to look. But she's bad sick."

"I'll find her."

"I'll bring you some turkey dinner if I can. Some leftovers."

His eyes sparkled. "That'd be real nice."

Cirri got up. "I'm gonna take a bath."

"So what about this fight?"

She walked past him. "None a' your business."

Heck

MINI-STROKES, TRANSIENT IS-
chemic attacks, Heck's doctor had told him. Yes, they would
have accounted for the blurriness, for the weakness on one
side, for some degree of erratic behavior. His blood pressure
was too high. He was either having clots in the vessels of his
brain or was developing atherosclerosis. He'd have to come in
for further tests, but, in any case, the best treatment was to
keep the pressure down.

There was no point in keeping him in the hospital. Usually
that just increased a patient's blood pressure. He should go
home, take it easy, and let the medicines do their work.
They'd set up an appointment for tests later.

Sometimes mini-strokes preceded a larger stroke, sometimes not. There was no way of knowing. But his doctor had
seen the medications do wonders.

Heck sat on the bed, waiting for the discharge papers, and

for Tina to call from the lobby that she had the car pulled up in front. Yvonne had come in early to hear the doctor's instructions and to pack up the few things she'd brought him from home. She insisted that he not walk in the rain. He had made a fuss. "Of course, I can walk fifty yards in the rain. My problem is not going to be made worse by rain, not even cold rain."

But secretly, he was glad. He was so tired. A hospital was no place to rest. The nurses had been in to bother him every couple of hours all night long—taking his temperature, his blood pressure, giving him pills. And then he'd lain there trying to get back to sleep, thinking about how all this was going to affect his future.

Surely the family would excuse him for a little nap later today. On the other hand, though, he hated to miss any of their Thanksgiving time together. Except for Edward, in Ceylon, and Hector Junior, who was on call this weekend, the rest of the children would be home. Katie hadn't planned on coming home, but under the circumstances, she had hopped the train in Wellesley last night.

Yvonne looked at her watch.

"You're wanting to get that turkey in, aren't you?" Heck said, eager to talk of ordinary things.

"No. John said he'd do it for me. I stuffed it last night."

"After you left here? That was late."

She was in her geared-up, worried frame of mind. Whenever there was a crisis—sickness, money problems, trouble with the kids—she got into a panicky rush. He thought this was because she figured she hadn't been working hard enough to keep trouble at bay. Now that it was here at their door, she had to work harder.

Ever since he'd called her yesterday from the emergency room and she'd come racing over from work, she'd worn a tight, harried expression. She had to be on guard. She had to be thinking, preparing, doing something every minute to hold their lives together.

He had the opposite response to crisis. It made him slow down. A brush with danger or trouble made him stop and analyze and appreciate. He knew this face that Yvonne wore, for instance. He'd seen it a hundred times. But in this particular moment, he saw it fresh, saw the beauty in her determination and concern, saw, too, the fragility of it. Because no one could really prevent trouble from coming. Everybody had to endure a certain amount of pain. That was life. And they'd been luckier than most.

"Well, then, I guess John has gotten it in the oven all right," he said.

"And then he's going to pick Katie up at the station. I hope the train is on time. It's so hard to park around there. And with all this weather."

"He's all grown up, baby. He'll figure it out."

"Well, then, where's Tina? She should have been able to get the car by now."

"Can't leave till those discharge papers come anyway."

She got up and headed to the door. "I'm going to see if the nurse can't hurry those up. You be okay?"

"I'll be fine."

He took this moment to close his eyes and ease the stinging. Then the phone rang.

"Daddy." It was Tina, and she was crying. "Some girl attacked me outside the hospital. I'm in the emergency room. They say I'm gonna need stitches."

"What girl?"

"My face is hurt."

Heck lowered his legs off the bed. "We'll be right down."

* * *

Her left cheek was split by a jagged cut. She had several other wounds, bloody and oozing, that the nurse revealed to them when she removed the gauze.

"Who did this?" Yvonne demanded.

Tina couldn't stop crying. "Some girl when I went to get the car."

Heck stooped down in front of her as she sat in the chair. "Do you know her?"

"I've seen her."

"Who is she?"

"I'm not sure."

"Quit lying to me!" Yvonne said.

Heck touched Yvonne's arm. "Does she go to Grant?"

Tina nodded.

"That girl we saw last night with those little kids," Yvonne said.

Tina glanced at her, looked away.

"I'm right, aren't I?"

Heck rubbed Tina's hand. "Who is she?" he asked quietly.

"Cirri James."

"Why did she do this to you?"

Tina started crying again. "I don't know."

"Why did she hurt you?" Heck asked softly.

"I don't know."

"Talk to your father. He's very sick. Why do you treat him like this? He should be at home in bed!"

"Because she thought I was going with her boyfriend, which I'm not!"

"You're telling me it's mistaken identity? What was the name she said last night? Marcus? Who is this Marcus?"

"Marcus Chance?" Heck asked.

Tina nodded.

"You been flirting with him?"

Tina shook her head.

"Then why did she think you were here last night to see Marcus?"

"I don't know."

"Why does she think you're dating him if you're not?"

"I don't know."

"You're lying again."

"I'm not! I don't know."

"Who *are* you seeing, then?" Heck asked.

Tina shook her head without looking at them.

"Your father asked you a question!"

Tina didn't answer.

"Why don't you want to tell us?"

"Is it that Marcus?"

"I told you it wasn't."

"Well, then who?"

"I'm not telling you."

"Why not?"

She set her lips and remained silent.

Yvonne drove him home and sent Katie and John to pick up Tina. The doctor had just started stitching her up when they left. Heck was too tired to wait. He was glad to be home.

Yvonne wanted him to go upstairs to bed, but he asked her to bring him a pillow and a blanket so he could stretch out on the couch. He wanted to be in their midst, especially now, when he was feeling so grateful and open to everyone. When he could see so clearly.

He and Yvonne had switched sides about Tina. Yvonne was furious with the girl. Heck could see Tina was floundering. She was in trouble, and he felt guilty. He'd spent his days try-ing to recognize danger signals in other students, but all the while he'd been missing them in his own daughter. He couldn't say what the trouble was, but he intended to find out, not by demanding, but by understanding—trying to see the pressures she felt that pushed her one way or another. Obviously, she was dating someone they wouldn't approve of. Otherwise, why wouldn't she have told them? Who was a boy he would least like to see her with? He ran through faces at school with their mustaches and their war stories about Oak Hill and Lorton, boys who came to school irregularly and spent the rest of their days running the streets. What would he say if she mentioned one of their names? Marcus Chance was an angel with wings compared to any of them.

But why *would* she want to go with any of them? He tried to understand her reasons and feelings. Same reason for the earrings, for her rejection of their values. She was acting out her independence. And her ingrown stubbornness made things worse.

He knew Cirri James only vaguely. What did she have to do with Tina's rebellion and the mystery boy? Where was she now, and how badly had she been hurt? He was sure that Tina was not all innocent in this fight. He could try calling Cirri. But the records were at school and James was such a common name, he'd never find it in the phone book. Tomorrow. He needed to get the story from Tina first.

Yvonne bustled down the stairs with two pillows and a comforter. She helped him off with his jacket, unlaced his shoes and fluffed the pillows while he eased onto the couch.

"I'm not an invalid," he said. "But you're taking very good care of me. I like it."

She tucked the comforter around him. "That child. I'm going to send her out of this house."

"Yeah? Where to?"

"Boarding school. A military academy. Siberia. I don't know. You and I don't need all that stuff she's putting down."

Yvonne cupped her hands around her temples. "Cut up, in the emergency room, on Thanksgiving Day, and you so sick. Last thing you need is upset."

He pulled her closer to the couch. "I don't feel upset. I feel very good, nice and comfortable here, smelling that turkey, and knowing my children are about to walk through the door."

She knelt down beside him. "I'm so scared for you, though."

"High blood pressure. I feel a world better." He rubbed her cheek with one finger. "He said that getting that pressure under control might just take care of it. Remember? No use thinking any worse."

The years had laid down sweet wrinkles around her mouth and across her forehead. But all the lines were looking worried today. She bent down and kissed him. Then she jumped up. "Gotta baste that bird."

The three kids came rushing in. Katie was striking, as always, in her long purple coat and suede boots. Her posture and movements were as elegant as a dancer's, and she radiated confidence. John was tall and slim: the responsible one who'd put the turkey in the oven and picked up his sisters—one at the station, one at the hospital—backing up his mother, quietly taking care of things. Tina's face was swollen, her eyes red from crying. She flung her wet coat on the bannister, as she usually did, as she'd been asked a thousand times not to do, and slunk up the stairs.

Katie hugged him and Yvonne. "Bad enough to be coming home because of one person in the hospital, but two!"

"Where'd she go?" Yvonne asked, looking for Tina.

"Upstairs," John answered.

"Daddy, what is this?" Katie asked, sitting beside him on the couch.

"Hypertension. That's all. It got out of hand."

"Mom said mini-strokes."

"You know how doctors are. Always looking at the worst."

"But you were having these episodes?" John asked.

"Felt strange a couple of times. Yesterday, I felt it coming on again—headache, blurriness, couldn't think straight. I said, 'This isn't right,' and just went ahead to the hospital."

"Hector Junior's calling us this afternoon," Yvonne said.

Heck smiled. "Useful to have a doctor in the family."

"And what's Tina's problem?" Katie asked.

"She wouldn't talk to us when we picked her up," John said.

"Was she in a fight?" Katie asked. "Is she running with some bad kids or something?"

"She won't talk to us, either," Yvonne said.

"Is she in trouble?"

Yvonne shrugged.

"She has no right to be putting you through this," said Katie.

"Let me tell you something," Heck said. "You all went through some rocky times 'bout this age. Things are worse at Grant now. Principal's not up to the job anymore."

"That's not true, Daddy. You've always been the best," Katie said.

"This is my last year. I told 'em yesterday I'm going to re-tire, effective in June."

"You did?"

He wanted to get off this subject. "Don't blame Tina. Maybe sometimes it seems that the baby's got it easier, but she's carrying a heavy load."

"You've *been* Grant all these years," Katie said. "What are you going to do? What will the school do without you?"

Heck hugged her. "We'll see."

* * *

They talked about their courses and schools, papers and exams coming up, friends, professors, the people they were dating. John had been going with the same girl for two years. She'd gone to New Jersey for the holiday. Katie giggled about a crush she had on a young man.

Heck felt the acute difference between all this and what Tina talked about with them, which was nothing. He hadn't realized how far away from them she'd grown. Yvonne was busy. He'd been preoccupied. The child had been on her own. Maybe they'd made her feel less valued, less loved. So she was out there doing all these things to get their attention and keeping everything to herself to get revenge.

He was sleepy. John and Katie were talking about graduate schools and scholarships. And he couldn't keep his eyes open.

He woke up sweating and threw back the comforter. The aroma of the turkey was overwhelming. His family was talking and washing up. The sounds were all familiar.

He got up slowly. Standing, he didn't feel shaky or dizzy or weak, just a little groggy. He made it up the stairs.

Tina was lying on her bed, staring at the ceiling. Not crying, not moving. There were no lights on, and because of the rain outside, the room was very dim. The stark white bandages on her face seemed to glow. Even when he approached her bed, she didn't move so that, for an instant, the thought flashed across his mind that she had killed herself.

"Tina."

She didn't move. His heart galloped. He seized her arm. Then she turned her head toward him. "You scared me," he said.

"Thought I was dead?"

He stared at her.

"Now you know how I felt that day."

"I wasn't pretending, though!" he said, shocked.

"I wish I wasn't, either. I wish I was dead."

"How have we gotten to this place, baby?" he asked, carefully lowering himself onto her bed.

"I don't know."

"That day when you found me downstairs on the floor, the things you said, it seemed like you still loved me a little bit."

She didn't respond.

"What is so awful that you can't tell us about? Whatever it is, I'll forgive you. I just want to help you, Tina."

A sob came from her, and it surprised him. She put her fingers gingerly over her eyes, careful not to touch the bandages.

"They give you anything for the pain?" he asked, realizing that the stitches must hurt.

"Uh huh."

"You take it?"

"No."

He noticed a bottle on the bedside table. "This it?"

"Uh huh."

He read the directions, shook out two pills, then went to the bathroom to get some water. When he came back, she was sitting up. He handed her the glass and the pills.

"It hurts," she whimpered.

He patted her leg. Then she leaned back against the pillows. "The boy is Nick Tiebault."

"He's white!"

She glanced up. "Is that a problem?"

"Not exactly, I guess. Only I thought you didn't want anything to do with black folks moving on up, trying to act like white folks, let alone actually going out with white folks."

"I know." She began crying again. "I don't understand it either. I'm so confused."

* * *

Heck tried to protect Tina from her brother and sister and even from Yvonne because they were all angry with her. Katie said it for all of them. "I just hate what she's doing to you, Dad."

They sat at the Thanksgiving table, lingering over decaf and pumpkin pie. Tina had come downstairs briefly for the meal and then retreated to her room.

"She's not doing anything to me," Heck said. "I can take care of myself. She's the one needs our help."

"She needs to be grounded for the rest of her life," John muttered.

"It's embarrassing," Katie said.

"Now, what's embarrassing?" Heck asked. "The fact that your sister got into some trouble? Or does that trouble signify something else to you?"

"It says 'low-life nigger,' " said Katie.

"Katie," Yvonne moaned.

"Well, it does. Why don't we say what we're thinking? We have always tried to rise above that, haven't we? Isn't that what you taught us? We can be better than those folks. Well, we've succeeded. And I refuse to have to worry about and be embarrassed by my spoiled baby sister who won't make the grade. We all went through the same stuff at Grant. It was hard. But I'm glad I did it. I'm glad I'm at Wellesley. It's a whole different life there."

"You can be almost white," Heck put in.

"That's right!" she shouted. "We share the same values. I'm appreciated there. I'm liked, maybe sometimes *because* of the color of my skin, but that doesn't bother me. I have more friends there than I ever had at Grant because so few people at Grant knew what to do to get out of this neighborhood or had the drive to do it. But you and Mom paved the way for us. I don't like to come back here. It scares me. And she should be glad to be able to get out too. I don't understand her problem."

"She doesn't either," Heck said. "She admits she's confused." He wanted to tell them about Nick Tiebault, but he didn't want to betray Tina's confidence, not even to Yvonne.

"All right. She can be confused. But she's got to do well in school at least. Mom says she's sloughed off to C's and D's."

"Maybe she's just not as bright as you kids were."

"Come on, Dad," Katie said. "She's been a brilliant manipulator all her life. And standards at Grant are shit. She can get D's just by showing up a couple times a week."

"Thanks," he said.

"You know what I mean."

"Yeah, I do. And if there's been some sloughing off, I have to take some of the blame for that at home, as well as in the school." He looked at Yvonne. "I think she's been trying to get our attention with all that behavior. I see it twenty times a day in school. But I missed it in my own daughter."

"You think it's drugs?" John said.

"I don't think so. Have you noticed anything, Yvonne?"

"I haven't."

"You two are going all soft about her again," Katie warned.

"There wouldn't be any jealousy toward your little sister in what you're saying, would there?" Yvonne asked.

"I'm not perfect. All I'm saying is there's a pattern here. You two are willing to make all kinds of excuses for her."

John, the diplomat-in-training, said, "I don't think it's helpful to argue about this. You both have good points. But you have different relationships with her, too. Each of us has to deal with her and this incident in our own way."

Heck stood up. "I think you're right, son. And that couch in there is calling for me."

Yvonne jumped up. "Let me help you."

"You sit. I'm fine."

Gratefully, he stretched out on the couch.

He was glad that things had come to a head with Tina. Now they could go forward instead of around in circles.

On the end table were the flowers that Danny had sent. He picked out three pink carnations and then climbed the stairs.

Tina was bent over the dresser, inspecting her wound in the mirror.

He touched her chin and turned it gently toward him. "Let me see. Looks clean. Looks like it's healing already."

"It's ugly."

"You gonna look like one of those African princesses with the ritual scars."

She turned away in disgust. "Stop, Daddy."

"No, we'll get it taken care of. The doctor gave you the name of a plastic surgeon?"

She nodded.

"We'll go see him."

She leaned back across the dresser to stare at the wound again.

"Brought you some flowers," he said. "We're the sick ones this weekend."

She sank onto the bed. He brought the flowers to her table. "You can look at them while you rest."

"Thanks."

He sat at the end of her bed and took one of her feet in his hands to massage it. "You been going with this Nick, right?"

She nodded.

"He good to you?"

She shrugged. The corners of her mouth were turned down.

"What do you like about him?"

"He's smart and he's smart-assed. He can make it at Grant even though he's white 'cause he's tough. He's bad, and I wanted to be tough too. I wanted to be smart-assed, too. Not some Katie Goody Two-shoes. So I liked him and he liked me. We were a pair. An' we egged each other on. We were tryin' to say 'Fuck you' to the system any which way we could."

"What system?"

"School, adults, this country that doesn't care about half of its people."

"But you're not together anymore?"

"I don't wanna be."

"Why not?"

"Let's just say he's doing some illegal crap. He's real involved in it. And I don't see the thrill anymore."

"Drugs?"

"Drugs, guns, you name it. He's gone someplace way beyond bad. He's someplace halfway to evil."

She wouldn't look at Heck. She had tightened up and pulled her foot away.

"When did you realize all this?"

"I *been* knowing it. In fact, I know too much."

"You think he might turn against you?"

"No tellin' what he might do."

"You doin' this drugs and stuff too?"

"I've smoked some stuff. It's easy to get. I'm not selling, though."

He gestured at her face. "You sure this wasn't part of it?"

"No. Weird as it is, this really was just some girl trying to protect her property. I been laying here thinking about it all this time. I don't think it was any more than that."

"Is there anything we can do about Nick? Get him some help?"

She snorted.

"Someplace we can catch him in the act, something . . ."

"There's one thing," she said, "but I don't know if you'd want to drag it up. Probably wouldn't get him too much time, either."

"What?"

She faced him. "He's the one messed up your office."

Heck's mind raced. The french-fry container on the desk, the broken glass, the condom. The door that had been unlocked, not forced. "And you?" He barely got out the words.

She stared at him.

"What was he after?"

"Nothing."

"How'd he get in?" She didn't answer. "How did he get in?" he repeated himself.

She bowed her head. "You always leave your keys on the table by the front door."

He couldn't talk to her anymore. His tolerance had vanished. He veered out of the room, went to his own bedroom and fell onto the bed. The room seemed to be spinning, but when he looked at the walls, he realized the spinning was only in his head.

She had stolen his keys, gotten into the building, and fucked the boy on his desk. Coolly, she had watched him go through the pain and anger and shock the office destruction had caused. For the thrill of it, she had slept with, smoked shit with, and did who-knew-what-else with this smart-assed punk. She was cruel and imbalanced in some way. She didn't know her own mind and couldn't see what was around her, or else she didn't care about what she saw, which was worse.

She'd told him about the office. But why? To get back at Nick, knowing all the time that she herself would probably be safe. Had she gambled on Heck's not wanting to drag her to the authorities? Her actions and reactions were all out of proportion. And constantly she calculated, manipulated, as Katie said, to keep herself as much in the clear as possible.

He should turn her in to the police. Would that shock her into some semblance of normalcy? She should feel the consequences of her actions. That was only right. They'd always been too lenient with her, sheltered her, made excuses for her, as Katie had said. He'd said downstairs that it was his fault for not giving her enough attention. No. Tina's problems were her own.

Just as he'd reached that conclusion, Tina barged into the room and threw herself on her knees beside the bed.

"Daddy, don't walk away from me," she sobbed. "Please don't turn your back on me. I never would have told you about the office. I never wanted to hurt you, but someone has got to stop him. I could quit him and I will, but that won't stop him." Her face was bloated and shiny. "He has runners all over the neighborhood. They're selling stuff right outside Grant. They have so much money. And they got guns. Nick's got a gun. He took it from Miz Brown's desk."

She clutched at his hand, but he jerked it away from her. "I been wrong," she wailed, burying her face in the bedspread. "I didn't want to hurt you. I love you, Daddy. Believe me. Help me!"

The noise brought Yvonne and the others to the room. He motioned them out, then stood up and closed the door.

"Come here!" he said, pointing to a spot on the floor.

She stood where he told her to.

"Get down on your knees."

She knelt.

"Hands behind your back!"

She did as he told her.

He walked around her. "I been in here thinking about sending you to jail. They'd put you in handcuffs and lock you up. What's the good of a life lived like that?"

He paced slowly around her.

"An' you let this smart-assed, white-trash, no-good punk enslave you. He fucked you just like some foreman, didn't he? On my desk. And he's probably bragging about how easy it was to get in the principal's daughter's pussy. Did he drag you down in the mud? Yes, he did. And he's dragging Grant and this whole neighborhood and whatever I been trying to do here for twenty-five years down in the mud, too, with his dope and his bloodletting. Oh, he's not the only one. I know that. But he's the only one who concerns me right now. Because you come in here crying about somebody's got to stop him. Okay, we'll figure something out.

"But what about you? That's what really bothers me. What happens when the next jive-assed son of a bitch comes along? You gonna lay down any old place he tells you and spread your legs then, too?"

She covered her face with her hands.

"Put your hands behind your back! Are you gonna turn your back on me and your mother and your whole family and everything we ever gave to you so you can show off how bad you are, to show how you can fit right into the neighborhood?"

He put his hands on her shoulders and shook her. "Look at me! We raised you to be different." Her face was bleeding under the stitches, but he kept shaking her. "Have you learned this lesson?" he yelled. "In the school of life, have you learned this, or am I sending you to prison?"

"I don't want to be a point for you. I just want to make my own life," she cried.

"Yeah. Poor white trash and poor nigger trash. Some life."

Yvonne rushed in then and pulled him away from her. "You're going to hurt her." He backed up and leaned against the door while Yvonne comforted their daughter. Then he slunk out of the room.

Cirri

CIRRI TOOK A HOT BATH, FIXED
her hair as best she could, and put on a blouse and skirt. Then
she braided Pea's hair and fixed Willie's twisted belt. She was
feeling fine. Marcus didn't love Tina. And Furry was going to
find Mama.

She'd take Mama back to the hospital and stay with her day
and night so Mama wouldn't leave again. She'd convince
Mama that no one was going to bother her, that the police
weren't after her, weren't going to break up the family. Furry
could stay with the kids. And maybe by Monday, Mama'd be
well enough to come home. Or maybe she wouldn't be afraid
of the hospital anymore, so Cirri could leave her and go on to
school, to see if she couldn't patch things up with Marcus.

The kids had raincoats with hoods. Cirri held a plastic grocery bag over her head as they walked to Thea's.

"They been nice enough to invite us. You gotta be nice

enough to behave," Cirri told them. "Thea's got a baby. Bryan. Maybe you can baby-sit him. An' use good manners."

"They gonna have pie?" Willie asked.

"They gonna have everything. I was over there when she was fixin' it."

"Whip cream?"

" 'Magine so."

"I want puddin' like we had at Marcus's house," Pea said.

"Don't generally have puddin' at Thanksgiving time," Cirri said.

"Oh, I forgot to tell you," Willie said. "Marcus said he'd come to see you later."

Cirri stopped. "What you mean?"

"Marcus come by when you was at the hospital this morning. And he said—"

"Why didn't you tell me?"

Willie looked at Cirri like she was deaf. "I forgot."

"What do you mean, 'you forgot'?"

"Furry was there. We were watching cartoons and playing with the kitty . . ."

"What he say?"

"Said he'd come over later."

"Later when?" Would he be coming there now?

"He said 'round about six o'clock," Pea put in.

"That's right!" Willie shouted.

"Six o'clock," Cirri repeated. "Lord a' mercy." She grabbed their hands and ran down the street. Then she stopped and jumped straight up. "Whooee! It's a Thanksgiving day!"

"You shoulda called me," Thea's father greeted them at the door. "I woulda picked you up in the car. It's no kinda day to be walking."

"Look at y'all." Thea came to the door carrying Bryan. "You swim here?"

"I woulda been glad to pick 'em up if they'da called," Mr. Williams said again.

"Without no phone, how they gonna call?" Thea told him. "Gimme them coats. I'll hang 'em in the bathroom."

Thea's mother hurried out from the kitchen, an apron around her broad stomach. "Well, I'm glad you came. Althea wasn't sure."

Cirri nodded. "I'm sorry. I couldn't say for sure. My mother's been sick."

"That's what Althea said."

"Yeah, an' she's in the hospital," Pea piped up. Willie elbowed her and put on his most ingratiating smile.

"Hospital! My heavens!"

"What's the problem?" Thea's father asked.

"Pneumonia," Pea said.

"She going to be all right?"

"Yeah," Pea went on. "Cirri was there to visit her this morning. An' a old friend of ours came home. He was burned outta his place by the hustlers, but he came back this morning and we named our kitten after him."

"Is that right?" Mrs. Williams said. "Well, I hope your mama's getting a good Thanksgiving dinner in the hospital 'cause she gonna be missing a good one here."

Emboldened by Mrs. Williams's friendliness, Pea asked, "Do you have whip cream for your pies?" Then she looked to Willie to prove that she had his best interests at heart.

"Let's see now, did I buy that whipped cream? You mean that kind that you shake and turn the can upside down and spray it out all over your pie?"

Pea nodded seriously. "Yeah, that kind."

"Did I buy that, Althea?"

"Quit playin' with them," Thea's father said.

"Yes, we got that kind," Thea said. "Maybe we should skip the turkey an' go straight to dessert."

They all moved into the living room where the kids found seats on the couch. The Macy's parade was on TV. Thea settled Bryan in her father's lap so she could go help in the kitchen. Cirri went too.

"They cute as puppies," Thea's mother said, stirring something on the stove.

"If that's Pea's idea of behaving," Cirri complained, "then she needs a hand to her behind."

"She's fine. Don't need nothin'."

Thea was arranging pickles and olives on a relish plate. Cirri stood beside her at the kitchen table.

"So did you find Marcus the other day?" Thea asked.

It seemed like weeks since Cirri had seen Marcus and Tina and Nick outside C & J's. With Mama so sick and everything else, she hadn't made all the connections until right now. But now she realized why the three of them had been standing there. Nick and Tina were together. Marcus was there because he and Nick worked the night shift. She had come to the wrong conclusion. And Marcus was coming to see her at six.

For the first time, she wondered how Tina was. Her face had been pretty well messed up, and she had been crying as she'd been helped into the hospital. All for a mistake. But Cirri wasn't too sorry. Tina had gotten in her wallops, too, and enjoyed it.

It was impossible to explain all this to Thea.

"How long your mama gonna have to stay in the hospital?" Mrs. Williams asked, not having heard Thea's question.

"Few days, I guess."

"That pneumonia's tricky. Stays with you a long time. My

mother had it last year. Double pneumonia. She was tired as a baby for months."

Thea was making the pickles into a star pattern and putting olives and pickled onions between the spokes. Cirri's mouth filled with water.

Mrs. Williams dribbled a molasses mixture over mashed sweet potatoes. Then she sprinkled on cinnamon and dotted it with little marshmallows. "Althea said you the main one holding things together over there. That's a hard thing. All you babies takin' on heavy responsibilities before your times."

Cirri's head was spinning. The cheek that Tina had hit throbbed. Mrs. Williams finished with the sweet potatoes, wiped her hands on her apron, and turned to Cirri. "Our church has a treatment program. And it's real good, I hear. Now, I don't mean to be sayin' nothin' that's not my business. But Althea's told me 'bout what-all you're doin', an' I'm sure your mama would rather be rid of that scourge than be livin' with it. An' nobody needs a junkie for a mother."

The only thing Cirri could think about was that everyone was calling her mother a junkie. The kitchen walls were caving in on her. She backed up a step, then tried to get hold of the table edge before she fell.

She sat down hard on her behind. Only then did she realize she'd pulled the tablecloth down with her. Thea's pickles and olives were scattered all over the floor.

The women screamed and bent over to help her. Mr. Williams rushed in with the baby. Pea and Willie were right behind him.

"What happened?"

"You all right?"

"Land sakes!" Mr. Williams boomed. "Stand back an' give her air."

"I'm okay," Cirri whispered.

Thea leaned in close and took Cirri's hands. "Come on, let me help you up. You tryin' to sit down? Can't you see they's no chairs here?"

"I'm just kind of hungry," Cirri murmured.

"Lord, chile. You make me so mad. We ain't got enough food in this room that you can't have a taste?"

Cirri felt embarrassed. She didn't like everyone staring down at her.

"She need some food? Goodness gracious." Mrs. Williams grabbed a buttered roll and handed it to Cirri.

Cirri looked at Willie and Pea. "I'm not behavin' too good, am I? After all I told you."

"No. An' lookit this mess!" Pea said indignantly.

"Aw, that ain't nothing," Mr. Williams said and stooped to pick up the pickles. "Help me out here. You're closer to the ground than I am."

Thea helped Cirri into the dining room. She pointed to Cirri's cheek. "Where you get this? I just noticed it."

"Don't bother me while I'm eating," Cirri complained, not wanting to think about all that again.

Mrs. Williams came in with a plate. "Here's some cheese and fruit salad. I'm hurrying up the potatoes. You shoulda said you were hungry."

"I'm sorry about the relish plate," Cirri said.

Mrs. Williams flapped her hand. "I don't like that stuff anyway. Just do it for company."

"You messed up my arrangement," Thea said, laughing.

Cirri gratefully started in on the cheese.

"Lord of heaven and earth." Mr. Williams prayed while the turkey steamed under his extended hands. "The harvest has been gathered for another year and we come to thank you for its bountifulness. Our young friend Willie here says we said *chakula* for 'food' when we were in Africa. So let's say it now, too."

"*Chakula*," everyone chimed in.

"We also know that this day commemorates the humble beginnings of this country, when people sat down as brothers and sisters to thank You for a good year, with hopes that You would hold them in Your bosom for yet another year to spare them and guide them. We need sparing and guiding now no less than they did then."

"Amen," Mrs. Williams said.

"We live in a hurtin' world, in a hurtin' town. We try our best but we need Your help too. Stand by us, Lord!"

"Uh huh!"

"This is also a day of families getting together all over this land. Without the joy and help and love in families, we would all be lonely wayfarers out in the cold and the wet, wondering about why we were put here. In a family we get love and meaning in our lives."

"Yes, Lord."

"An' we're thankful for friends, our young friends here sharing our table, bringing their innocence and vitality into this household."

He took a deep breath. "Finally, bless this food to the nourishment of our bodies. Watch over these children to keep them out of harm's way and make Your light to shine in their lives. A-men."

"A-men."

After all the food, they played Bingo, Blindman's Buff and Hide the Thimble. For each game, Mrs. Williams had threatened that the loser would have to do the dishes. With the stakes that high, a lot of suspense was focused on winning. Cirri couldn't remember seeing Pea and Willie so involved. They threw themselves into every game; the whole house seemed to throb with their high spirits. Several times Mr. Williams winked at Cirri and laughed at whatever the kids were doing, he was enjoying their enthusiasm so much.

Later, Cirri and Mrs. Williams and Thea worked on the kitchen. But it hardly felt like work. They nibbled before they wrapped the food and put it away. They talked while they scraped and washed and dried the dishes. It was easy talk, sprinkled with teasing and stories about folks they knew.

In the car, when Mr. Williams drove them home, Cirri scolded Willie for having three helpings of pie.

"Well, she offered it," Willie said.

Mr. Williams chuckled. "And goodness knows, we don't need no extra pie sitting around this week. We all trying to be on diets."

Cirri held a covered plate of turkey and dressing and gravy on her lap. Mrs. Williams said it would be tomorrow's lunch, and Cirri had thanked her, but she meant to give it to Furry.

The closer they got to home, the more jittery she got. As the windshield wipers slapped back and forth in the gloom, she felt all the old worries descend on her again like a heavy cloak. She'd been able to get out from under them for a while at Thea's, but now the demons were at her again, and her nerves spiked up.

What would they have to do with Mama tonight? How could they get her back to the hospital? Would the hospital take her after she'd walked out? What would she do with the kids while she took Mama back?

At least she'd have Marcus to help her tonight. She would be embarrassed for him to see Mama so messed up, but what other choice was there? Marcus would come at six, wouldn't he?

And Furry would have found Mama, wouldn't he?

There were flashing lights up ahead. "Looks like fire

trucks," Mr. Williams said. They all craned to see as the car crept forward.

Three fire trucks crowded the street. Swarms of men rushed about in their helmets and heavy black coats. The street and broad concrete sidewalk in front of their building was criss-crossed with hoses, and the concrete glistened with standing water. A crowd of people—some of them residents of the building—huddled a little ways off.

"Which one is your house?" Mr. Williams asked.

Firemen were going in and out of the front door. "That one," Cirri said, fear rising in her.

A policeman flagged the car away from the curb and sig-naled Mr. Williams to move on. He rolled down his window. "These children live in that building. Is it safe to go in?"

"What floor?"

"Third," Cirri shouted.

"Fire was on that floor. I'll have to ask. Stay here." He moved toward a knot of firemen.

Cirri panicked. Mama had talked about how she owed the hustlers. "Wait!" she said, then burst out of the car and ran af-ter the policeman. "Wait a minute! What number was it? What house number?"

The policeman looked to a man who was wearing a uniform with a badge that read CHIEF. "Three nineteen," he said.

Cirri put her hand to her mouth. "That's my apartment."

"Where have you been?"

"Thanksgiving at a friend's. They just bringing me home. Me and my brother and sister."

She expected him to say, "*Good thing you weren't in there.*" But he didn't. Instead he muttered to one of his men. "Might have turned out different if they'd been there. Go get some-one who can talk to her."

Then Furry ran up. He had his hands folded together as if

he were praying. "Oh Cirri, this is a awful day. I never woulda brought her home. I just didn't know they was out for her."

"You found Mama?"

He nodded. "I carried her up all them stairs and left her on the bed, sleeping like a baby."

"She was in the fire?" Cirri yelled.

No one answered her.

"Was she?" she screamed.

"Yes," the chief said finally. "There was a lot of smoke. We couldn't revive her."

"What are you telling me?"

The chief spun around. "Get that social worker! Who's gonna take care of these children? Right now! I mean right now!"

Men scattered, running.

Cirri looked at Furry. "Do they mean she's dead?"

Furry didn't raise his head.

When a social-worker lady showed up in all the confusion and told Cirri that she and the kids would have to spend the night in a foster home, Mr. Williams pushed through the crowd and said that there'd be no such thing. They had a home to go to and it was his.

Cirri let him lead her and the kids back through the crush to his car. She was angry, but there was no one to be angry at except herself for her failure to do anything to save Mama. She shouldn't have been eating and enjoying herself all day. She should have been out looking for her. She should have been there when Furry brought her home. But what could she do now? The anger lodged in her throat. She wasn't sure if she wanted to scream or sob.

Furry followed them. "I'm sorry," he kept mumbling. "I'm sorry."

It wasn't his fault, but she couldn't talk. When they got to the car, she handed him the plate of food which she'd saved for him.

"Mr. Williams," Pea cried suddenly and pulled on his jacket. "Our kitten's in there."

"Land sakes, Pea. Maybe it got out okay," he said.

"I'll look for it for you, Pea. I'll keep my eyes out for it. I surely will," Furry promised as Pea and Willie scrambled into the car. Just as Cirri was getting in, she saw Marcus pushing through the crowd.

"God, Cirri," he said when he reached her.

"I'm going to Thea's."

He took her hand. It seemed as if her hand in his was the only part of her that could feel anything. But Mr. Williams was starting the car, asking all the spectators to move. The rain had started coming down hard again. Cirri pulled away from Marcus and closed the door.

The next morning, Thea's mom didn't go to work so she could help out with all the arrangements. Mostly she answered the telephone and then relayed the information to Cirri who moved around the kitchen in slow motion getting cereal and toast for the kids. "There's gonna be an investigation by the fire department and the police. That's the third incident of arson in your building," Mrs. Williams told her.

The phone rang again. "No, they're here for the time being," Cirri heard Mrs. Williams say. "Well, I don't know 'bout all that. It's a better home than they been havin' for a while. Three bedrooms. They's seven of us now. I'd have to talk to my husband."

Pea and Willie weren't saying much of anything. That was fine with Cirri. She knew how they felt. She didn't feel like talking either. They ate their breakfast and listened to Mrs. Williams's side of the conversation.

Between calls, she complained. "Never did bother about you when you was livin' in all that trouble. Now all of a sudden, they gotta have everything all legal-like and keep track of every second."

Another call. "No, there haven't been any arrangements made yet. The morgue called this morning." She pulled the phone cord around the corner into the dining room, but Cirri could still hear her whisper. "The body's gonna be held for a while. Autopsy. It's all under police investigation."

Cirri looked out the window. The rain had stopped, but the sky was still gray. She couldn't convince herself it was true. Didn't she still need to be worrying about Mama out in the cold? Wouldn't they go back to their house and find Mama shivering and shaking in the bed, glad to see them? She'd fix Mama some eggs and bacon and toast and warm milk and they'd take a cab to the hospital and find Dr. Brunson, and Mrs. Williams would contact the treatment center at the church, and Pea and Willie and herself would go shopping to buy blouses and skirts for Mama for Christmas. That would be a fine Christmas. A soft pink blouse with some kind of nice stitching on the collar and a pair of pearl earrings. Mama used to have pearl earrings that looked so nice on her.

"I imagine the woman don't have any clothes to be buried in," Mrs. Williams was whispering. "Oh, that would be kind of you."

Cirri's throat got so hard she couldn't swallow. Just then Bryan started crying. "Come here to Mama," said Thea, picking him up. She kissed and hugged him, and he settled down right away.

Pea stuck her thumb in her mouth and curled up on Cirri's lap. Cirri put her arms around her. Then Willie started crying. He bent over his cereal bowl and cupped his hands around his face. There were no tears, just his shoulders heaving. Cirri wished she could help him or hold him, but there was no more she could do. He was on his own.

After lunch, Mrs. Williams went to work. Thea and Bryan took a nap, and then Pea and Willie fell asleep watching TV. Cirri looked at the TV, but the images made no sense. She couldn't follow the story.

When Marcus showed up at the door, he wouldn't come in. He just stood with his head down, not even looking at her at first.

"This ain't no time for me to be comin' around," he said. "Your mom. I don't hardly believe it. I know you must be feeling bad." He glanced at her, then sideways down the street. "I treated you bad, Cirri. An' I'm sorry. Her on the stuff and you tryin' it. I just didn't want it to be a thing 'like mother, like daughter.' You know?"

She swallowed, hardly able to make sense of his words.

"I love all kinds of things about you. But the thing that really says somethin' to me is how you are with them kids. Your love goes deep. That means a lot."

He held out an envelope to her. "I know you gonna be needing some money. Take this. An' when you feel like talkin', you know where I'll be. Mimi's. Right? She got a phone there. You can call."

She nodded.

"You okay?"

She tried to smile. "I don't know."

"You care for me at all?"

She nodded again, unable to do more.

He stepped up and kissed her. "That's all I needed to

know." Then he backed down the stairs. "Call me anytime. If you want to."

She sat for a long time on the couch watching the soap operas. Finally, she lifted the flap of the envelope. There were fives, tens, twenties. Lots of them.

The money didn't make her happy. Didn't make her feel relieved. Didn't make her wonder where it came from. All she knew was that it was sitting in an envelope on her lap.

Marcus said he'd treated her bad, that he loved her. So how could one mistake have gotten in the way of all that love? His hurting her and her fight with Tina were all wrong. But he loved her. That was good. Because she loved him, too.

She ran her fingers over the edges of the bills. What use was all this money? It was Marcus's love that she cared about. It was Pea and Willie she cared about, and they were being taken care of right here in this house.

On TV someone was having a baby, and someone else was fighting with the nurse. It made no sense.

She looked over her shoulder at the bookcase. Then she got up, and sat down crossed-legged on the floor in front of the books. She took out a book and stuck a twenty-dollar bill somewhere in the middle of it and replaced the book on the shelf. She kept doing that again and again until the envelope was empty.

Danny

DANNY GROANED WHEN THE radio clicked on at five o' clock Monday morning. Heck had called and asked her to come to school earlier than usual. But she didn't want to face life yet. She rolled over and groped for the comforter, allowing herself five more minutes in bed. In the background, the weatherman was stupidly cheerful. The day was going to be warm and sunny, a break in the rainy spell they'd been having. Might even reach sixty degrees. "Put away the umbrellas and winter coats. Today is sweater weather!"

She reached out and struck the radio, and the weatherman shut up. What was there to be so goddamned cheerful about? It was dark, it was Monday. Five grueling weeks till Christmas vacation. The kids would all be in shitty moods, not wanting to be back at school, and she'd have to do handstands to get them involved.

She threw off the blanket and stumbled into the bathroom,

turned on the shower. Only water, plenty of it, on her head, would rouse her.

Her brain began to function, playing out the past and future in long ticker tapes. When Heck had called last night, Guy had answered the phone because she'd been in the bathroom.

"What's that bum doing at your house?" Heck said when she got on the line.

She'd pulled the phone into the other room and closed the door so Guy couldn't hear. "He's not a bum," she whispered.

"You still think he was responsible for your office?"

"No. What's he doing there?"

"Talking. This is my business, you know."

"He's not right for you."

"Thank you, Dr. Dating Service. But why are you concerned about this? How are you? That's what I want to know."

"I'm fine."

"Fine? Last I heard, you were in the hospital."

"I came home Thursday morning. I'm fine."

"What was wrong?"

"I got your flowers. Thanks a lot."

"What is it you're not telling me? Something embarrassing, like hemorrhoids or prostate?"

He chuckled. "It's a long story. The hospital's only the beginning. Could you meet me at school early tomorrow? Before seven?"

"Okay."

"Did you hear about Cirri James?"

"Cirri? What happened?"

"Her mother died in a fire on Thanksgiving."

"Oh, God. No. I haven't been reading the papers. She'd said her mother was sick."

"She was in the hospital same time I was. Now, go get that convict out of your house."

"Hey, it's my private life."

Guy had come to say good-bye. She had had an inkling he would. The hard part was that he'd had the decency to do it in person. He had built a fire in the fireplace and played a couple of games of chess with Rolls while she drank and threw together some spaghetti and salad. They had eaten in front of the fire.

When Rolls went to take a shower, Guy sat forward on the couch. "Cheryl and me are getting back together," he said abruptly. "I guess you were right to be jealous of her. And for giving me shit about her."

It didn't hurt as much as she thought it would. She wished she could make it easier for him. She wanted to say something light to let him know it was okay. But she couldn't seem to think of anything.

He leaned back. "I really do like you, Danny. You're a helluva lady. And you've been good to me. But like you said, I guess I still love Cheryl. An' I gotta go with that. We been together a long time. She knows me." He shook his head and laughed. "She's a bitch. We're gonna have some royal fights, I know. Shit. I'm sorry."

He'd done a pretty good job of apologizing, she thought. She held up her palms in a gesture of *C'est la vie!* "I enjoyed it while it lasted. And you were terrific with Rolls."

"He's a nice kid." He stood up. "Well, if you want me to take him out somewhere sometime . . ."

"To shoot things?"

"You didn't care for that, did you?"

At the door, when he was halfway to the truck, she shouted, "Stay outta trouble!"

"Right!" he yelled back.

It wasn't so much that he was *the* one, she'd concluded. But he'd given her the confidence that someone out there might be, and that she should try again. The guy didn't even have to look like Royce. She knew now that she and Rolls could take it.

The shower had done its job. She was awake.

Rolls wanted to have breakfast with her even though it meant getting up an hour earlier. So she woke him, then rushed around getting ready because, true to form, she was running late. She put out the pitiful cold cereal for him and slugged down a cup of coffee.

By the time he dragged into the kitchen, she felt under full sail. "It's going to a be a beautiful day," she told him. "Sunny and sixty. Believe that? After all this rain?" God, she was as obnoxious as the radio announcer.

He lifted one eyelid at her in disbelief.

"Okay. Got your gym shorts out of the dryer?"

"Yeah."

"Got your book report?"

"Yeah."

"Your lunch is here."

"Mom, I'm buying today. Remember? I told you."

"Ah yes! Cheeseburgers today."

"Bingo," he said.

She grinned at his tousled, sleepy head. He *was* a good kid.

"Guess what?" she said, picking up her book bag, kissing the top of his head.

"You're late."

"Right! I love you. See you after school."

She figured Heck wanted to talk to her about Cirri. But how did it involve her? Wasn't there family to step in? Where was Cirri's father? Wouldn't social services be engaged, if nothing else? Why should Heck be taking this on? Yvonne had talked about mini-strokes and high blood pressure. He wouldn't admit to being sick, but he should be taking it easy. Danny meant to tell him so.

He met her at the door and let her in because security wasn't there yet. As they climbed the stairs to his office, she noticed that his breathing was labored. "Heck, why are you here? You want to be the martyr of Grant High School? You're just out of the hospital. Go home and rest, for God's sake," she scolded him.

He unlocked his office and turned on the lights. She looked around, glad to see everything back in place. "I might leave early," he said. "I am a little tired this morning." He waved her to a chair. "Danny, I'm going to ask a favor of you."

"Anything. But then will you go home?"

"Tina was in a fight during the holiday. Her face is pretty cut up."

"Oh my God! What happened?"

"You wouldn't believe it if I told you. I'm making her come to school today even though she doesn't want to, you understand. You've got her first period . . ."

"Yeah. Cirri James is in there too. And after the fire . . ."

"Cirri's in there? Oh, Christ!"

"What?"

"Well, she probably won't be in school today anyway."

"Heck, what's going on?"

"I just wanted you to keep the kids off Tina's back, tell them it's none of their business. She *is* going to make it through this day."

"Heck, what is going on? Who did she fight with?"

"Cirri James. Over a boy named Marcus. But Tina was really going with Nick." Heck looked exhausted.

"Nick! I thought I kept up with the romances pretty well.

But that's a surprise. And he's in that class too." She scowled. "He's no winner."

"Nick is in that class?"

"Sure. They're my bright group."

"There's gonna be a police thing going down here today, too."

"Who are they after?"

"Nick."

"Wait a minute. Are you trying to tell me this is going to happen in my classroom this morning? Is this a 'Welcome back and thanks for the flowers'?"

Heck nodded wearily. "I didn't realize they were all in your class."

"Why are they after Nick?"

"For one thing, he smashed this office. He and Tina." He paused, giving Danny time to absorb the information. "For another thing, he's a heavy dealer. We're gonna clean up today. Maybe Marcus is in on it, too, but I'm pretty sure I got him on the straight and narrow. 'Least, I want to think I did."

"Get the school all cleaned up, get your daughter straightened out, and still go home early. It's gonna be quite a day."

His eyes pleaded with her. "I'd like you to keep Tina out of harm's way. Lord knows she's fucked this up, but she swears she's changed. I'm not sure I believe her. I can't stand the sight of her right now, actually. But Yvonne . . . I promised Yvonne we'd help Tina through this. Get her out on the other side."

"When's all this gonna happen?"

"I swear I don't know. If I did, I'd tell you. It's some kind of coordinated action with undercover cops and all. They promised me the least disruption."

"And what if I have all four of them in my class this morning? There's going to be a little tension in there."

"Tina's gonna be placid as a baby. She's promised heaven

and earth. And the others?" He grinned. "Since when do we
ever have good attendance?"

Heck was partly right. Lots of kids were absent, including
Nick, who usually arrived early. Danny wondered if he'd
somehow learned of the police action. Maybe through Tina?
Tina and Nick on Heck's desk. . . . Danny felt sorry for Heck
and Yvonne. Rolls had messed up, sure, but never so pointedly
against her. But then he wasn't seventeen, either.

Tina sat in a far seat by the windows. Her face was puffy
and she'd styled her hair so that it came forward around her
cheeks, but still the stitches were visible. She looked at no
one, met no one's eye. She concentrated on the closed books
stacked on the desk in front of her. Once in a while she
glanced up to see who came into the room. When Cirri and
Marcus walked in, she quickly turned to look out the window.

Evie slammed down her books. "What happened to your
face, girl?"

Tina dismissed her with a glare. "My Thanksgiving turkey
fought back."

Danny watched the exchange, ready to come to Tina's aid,
but she didn't need the help. Evie backed off. Tina always
managed to handle herself just fine.

Cirri carried no books or purse. She held Marcus's hand and
he led her to a seat as if she were blind, pulling his chair right
up next to hers. He brushed her hair back from her eyes and
put his arm around her in a comforting way. She seemed un-
aware of her surroundings. Danny tried to imagine the world
through Cirri's eyes: school as a distraction, a refuge. The
only solid, predictable thing in Cirri's life. Here was a room
full of raw potential and raw pain. How could she supply each
of these thirteen individuals with even a fraction of what they
needed?

Then Anya rushed in. "I've got to tell you something."

Danny felt overwhelmed. She couldn't even think about one more needy child with a problem. "You'll be late for your first-period class."

"Gimme a pass. It's about my parents."

"No, I'm not going to give you a pass."

"It's important!"

Danny inspected Anya's face. Aside from the oil and pimples and filthy teeth, there were no obvious bruises or injuries. She gestured to her class. "I've got to get started. Come talk to me at lunchtime."

"It's good news!" Anya insisted.

"Lunchtime"

The girl ran out.

She looked at the class. Everyone was subdued. The early hour, the end of the vacation, the horror that some of them had been through was a quieting force.

What could she do in fifty minutes to ease the burdens they carried at this moment? How to connect with them to let them know she cared? How to give them something in this vulnerable time that would last, would help them later on? How to demonstrate to them that they were valued, respected, loved, and not just society's refuse? Otherwise, how else would they value themselves?

She opened the book to the page she had planned to work on today. The correct use of quotation marks. The five-minute warm-up. Completely irrelevant.

Then why was Cirri here? Why had Heck insisted Tina come? Why had Marcus led Cirri to a chair in her classroom? They need the order, the routine, the discipline, the firm, steady touch. Quotation marks were irrelevant, but the process was not. Where else in their lives would this happen? What else could they count on absolutely but the cadence of

classes? While they were here there was a chance that someone might help them. As long as they were in this building
they were protected and guided. They came for the fifty-
minute rhythm of normalcy and routine.

She clapped her hands. "You're all looking so pitiful. But I
know just what'll perk you up. Page one twenty-two. Quotation marks!"

They groaned and complained in the usual way. "I know. I
know. It's not as much fun as semicolons, but, hey, it'll have to
do. Got used to sleeping late. Now you have to be here first
thing in the morning. Just stick your head under the faucet of
these quotation marks. Whoo! They'll wake you right up!"

"The whole page?" someone moaned.

"The whole shebang. Five minutes."

"Five minutes!"

"Is there an echo in here?"

"Why do we got to start out like this?" someone asked.

"Builds character. And I know you want lots of that, Ramon. Girls love character."

Ramon snickered and bent over his book.

She crossed her arms and wandered around the classroom
as they worked, commenting to each of them quietly.

"Your family put in too much hospital time this weekend,
didn't they?" she whispered to Tina.

The girl absently touched her stitches. "I guess so."

"I'm glad you and your father are okay. It's a fresh start today." Danny tried to keep it light, yet remind Tina that Danny
really didn't care what the past contained, as long as things
were better now.

Cirri looked up when Danny approached. Her eyes were
scared. "I heard about your mother. I'm very sorry. Is there
anything you need? Anything I can do?"

Cirri mashed her face into Marcus's shoulder. Marcus put

his hand around her head. "Take good care of her," Danny said.

She went to the window, stared out down the hill and across the city. All the familiar sights were there: the Capitol, the monuments. Then she turned and looked at the kids.

The class went on uneventfully. They corrected one another's punctuation papers. She talked to them about the play they were going to study, and with assigned parts they read some of it in class. Nothing out of the ordinary happened until one minute before the bell when Nick's face appeared briefly in the window of the closed door. He looked at her, scanned the class, then disappeared. She didn't know if anyone else had seen him; they were all reading the lines.

After class, she locked her door and hurried to Heck's office. He was on the phone, but he covered the mouthpiece when she came in.

"Nick's in the building, but he didn't come to my class."

"I know," Heck said. "We've just found out he's after Marcus. The police are going to get here at noon."

Her worries started bearing down on her. She wished Heck had never told her anything. Not about Nick, in the first place, not about the fact that he was out for Marcus. Certainly not the time, though she'd asked him for that information earlier.

She wondered if they were offering Marcus any protection. But why was Nick out to get Marcus anyway? That must mean that Marcus was in on the ring too. So wouldn't the police want to arrest Marcus as well? Danny had an image of Cirri sitting in class, attached to Marcus as if he were her lifeline. What was Cirri going to do without Marcus?

And, Heck had said that Tina and Nick were involved. Was

that over now? Had she turned him in? None of this was pretty.

She went to her office at lunchtime. The janitors had fired up the old boilers, apparently without listening to the weather report. The small, cramped room was stifling. Even with the door open, it was unbearable. She pushed up the window, then sat down at her desk to worry.

Nick could be anywhere in the building, hiding. How would they know where to look?

Anya strolled in. "You have time for me now?"

"Sure."

"My mom and dad are getting married."

"What?"

Anya smiled, revealing the green slime on her teeth. "They're getting married."

"You mean they haven't been married all this time?"

"They eloped and got married by a judge. Now they're gonna have a church wedding. They said it'll make 'em be better to each other."

"What do you think?"

"I think it's great. I get to be maid of honor."

Nick's voice, heard through the open window, interrupted Anya's story. In a singsong he said, "Marcus, honey, where's my money?"

Danny jumped up and peered outside, but couldn't see anyone. She hurried into the hall and ran toward the front door. All she could think of was Cirri, attached to Marcus's arm.

"Hey, where you going?" Anya shouted.

"Anya, stay here!" she yelled over her shoulder.

Heck was on the steps along with one of the security guards, surveying the kids milling around outside. Troops of them were heading down to C & J's.

"Around the corner," Danny pointed, winded. "Nick's around the corner."

The guard reported into his walkie-talkie. Heck took off down the steps. Somewhere a rap song was playing, the beat strong and heavy.

Behind her, she heard Anya. "Hey, what's going on?"

She whirled. "I told you to stay in the building!"

Marcus and Cirri were standing by a tree at the gym entrance. "Cirri James, go to the school office right now!" Heck barked. The force of his words pushed her away from Marcus. "There's Mrs. Mitchell. Go with her," he said.

When Cirri hesitated, he snapped, "This instant!"

This time Cirri went to Danny.

"I thought we had an agreement," Danny heard Heck saying to Marcus. "I thought I could count on you to get yourself on the right track." His voice was level, but Danny could hear the defeat and disappointment in it.

A shot rang out, so close she instinctively ducked. Someone behind her screamed. She looked around to see Anya crying and running toward her. Cirri shouted, "Marcus!" and started toward him. But Danny grabbed her and pulled her down onto the sidewalk.

Anya clutched at Danny. "I don't want to die!" she cried as Danny pushed her down too.

She glanced up. Nick stood only a few feet away, a gun in his hand. "Gimme my money, Marcus!" he yelled.

Heck walked slowly toward Nick. "Leave the boy alone," he said. "We can work this out. Get out of the business now, you won't have much time to do."

"Move, Jasper!" Nick shouted.

"No more wounds. No more blood. I'll help you out," Heck said. "I'll help you both out. I can do it. Believe me."

But Nick wasn't listening. He backed off a few steps and took aim at Marcus.

Heck yelled, "No!" He stepped in front of Nick, and the gun went off. The sound ricocheted off the walls of the school and echoed along the streets, louder than thunder, more piercing than a scream. Heck stumbled two more steps, his arms outstretched, as if to stop the shot. Then his feet crossed, and he fell.

At first, Danny thought he had tripped, a clumsy, awkward pratfall she would tease him about later on. Sirens screamed in the distance as Nick fled and Marcus ran to Cirri. And still Heck lay motionless, his feet crossed and his arms splayed out on the pavement as if they no longer had anything to do with his body. It wasn't until Danny saw the blood seeping from beneath Heck's chest that she realized he'd been shot.

Leo

DR. LEO CANALETTI SAT IN the tenth row of Holy Redeemer, the oldest Catholic church in Washington. Flanked on one side by the elementary school and on the other by the graveyard, it represented an earlier way of life. Once, the children had been baptized and confirmed in the church. They had passed through the grades of the elementary school and attended the Jesuit high school up the street. They had been married in this church, had their own children baptized here, and eventually had been laid to rest next to its walls. It had been a simple but effective system for simpler times. Apparently, the parents who now sent their children to the elementary school still hoped it worked.

On school days between eleven-thirty and one o'clock, the street in front of the church was blocked off so the children could play. They strung a volleyball net between two No Parking signs. They put down bases for kickball. They jumped ropes and played tag. But Canaletti had heard from the priests who served the parish that there were problems: single-parent families, suicidal teenagers, foul-mouthed third-graders, experimentation with alcohol and drugs, violent fights. Times had changed. No school or institution was immune. He'd been coming to the church every day since Dr. Jasper's murder because the killing had shocked and frightened him. He needed a quiet place to think things through.

He came to early mass, then stayed on while the rugs were vacuumed and the flowers changed, while the kindergartners came in to practice lining up in front of the altar and singing their Christmas carols. Some days the priest came down to talk. Other days he did not. He'd granted Leo the privilege to sit as long as he wished.

The church was comforting. Familiar, like an old friend. It felt good to be there, much better than to be at his desk stacked high with problems, each more hopeless than the next. He vicariously felt the officiating priest's pleasure at reciting the ritual, with its timeless, never-changing, ever-beneficent themes. The monotony of the responses relaxed him and focused his thoughts. He hadn't been this meditative in years.

Dr. Jasper's funeral had been just the opposite: a Baptist service, noisy with weeping, gospel singing, and testifying mourners who got up and spoke about what the man had meant to them. The church had been overflowing. Many had stood out in the rain throughout the three-and-a-half-hour service. And still the former students, parents, neighbors, friends, hadn't wanted to let the casket leave the church. They had held on to it, cried on it, until the pallbearers had gently urged them away.

"He was a victim," the minister had said. "But he wouldn't want us to think of him that way. He wouldn't want to be a cold, passive statistic, just like no one else wants to be one. He would have said, 'Look at those two boys.' 'Cause that's how he was—always thinking of them children. 'One gonna be locked up a long, long time. An' the other one gonna be in there a shorter time but he gonna regret this day for the rest of his life. These boys were victims too,' he woulda said. 'Father forgive them,' he woulda said. That was the kind of man he was.

"There are a whole lotta victims out there. Little, bitty babies, born to addicted mothers, don't know why they twitch and hurt and feel so bad. Grade-school kids tryin' to make their way without guidance, without even food and clothes sometimes. Teenagers tryin' to act grown-up, tryin' to see the best way to live, an' we so rarely take the time to give 'em any ideas, to tell 'em they're fine people, like he did. Mothers and fathers, lost an' driftin'. We gotta help each other. That's what he said. He used to say, 'Don't forget the people, even the littlest ones.' An' he tried his best. At his school, in his neighborhood, in this city. He cared. Can we take some examples from him? What did he teach us? These are hurtin' times. He died tryin' to ease the pain. Can we learn from him?"

It was funeral-service talk, partly. Generous exaggeration to ease the pain of the family and friends. Dr. Jasper had been stubborn and angry, behind the times and defeated. Leo wondered how many of the mourners knew that Dr. Jasper had intended to retire in June because he'd given up, because the odds against success at Grant had become so enormous.

But still, the man had been dedicated and believed in what he was doing. He had worked as hard as he knew how for those kids, and a lot of people loved him for it.

How many mourners would there be at his own funeral? Leo wondered. What work had he accomplished that he'd truly believed in with all his heart? That was the question that frightened him.

Hector Jasper was the better man. Leo understood this now. In some way, he'd understood it all along, which was why he'd wanted to edge Jasper out. Issues of authority and hierarchy, right-thinking about solutions to problems, backgrounds, color, were all secondary to the fact that Jasper was a good man. It was correct that these things were said at his funeral.

Leo stretched his legs. He used to be able to sit still for much longer. He'd spent years doing scholarly research in a carrel in the silence of the library stacks, working on his Ph.D.; contemplative days of retreat before his ordination; long hours of dutiful desk work he had been assigned to by older priests when he was a novitiate. Then he had become restless and couldn't sit still anymore.

The sanctuary was not ornate, but simple, even drab. There were cracks in the bone plaster between the tall windows. The carpet runner down the main aisle was threadbare. The altar was plain white marble with a triptych—a lamb, a fish, the cross. He watched the play of light across the pews and ceiling.

When he'd offered his condolences to Mrs. Jasper before the service started, she had spoken to him with the moral authority of a woman who had partly died when her husband had died, and before that, had suffered when he'd suffered. Surely she knew about the disagreements he'd had with her husband. She was direct. "Heck had intended to go to the funeral of one of the school's parents," she said to him. "She died in a fire last week. I think with the autopsy and whatnot, things were held up. Ironically, her funeral is today, later this afternoon. I can't go. But I'm sure he would want you to go, under the circumstances. It would be educational for you."

"It's the least I can do," he had agreed, surprised at the odd request, but willing to comply.

Then she seemed to regret her attitude. "Thank you, Dr. Canaletti. I'd appreciate it."

That funeral had been a much smaller affair, held in a dismal, acrid-smelling funeral parlor near the school. The water- and mildew-stained dark purple walls hadn't been painted in years. The casket rested on a stand so rickety he was afraid it would collapse. The children sat up front, the oldest one, obviously the Grant student, sitting between the two younger ones. She had kept her head up, staring at the casket, while the little ones cried.

An older woman had introduced herself to him as Mimi Chance. "They are coming into my house," she told him, nodding toward the three children. "Foster care, for now. They gonna have a hard time for a while, don't you know. But I'll be glad of the company. I think my Marcus gonna be gone coupla years. He's a good child, but even the best going down the toilet these days."

Leo didn't know who she was talking about. He just nodded. The stench was making his eyes water.

Fortunately, the service—a couple of prayers, a psalm, a song performed by a member of the funeral parlor staff—was brief. He had gone home exhausted.

All he could think about that night was that Dr. Jasper would have attended that funeral. He would have taken the time and the emotional energy to go to that horrid place to sit with a handful of mourners. The woman had been lost in a fire. Tragedies happened every day. In a school community of that size, there were bound to be a hundred accidents or fires or deaths a year. Had Jasper felt it necessary to go to all of them? What was the point? The student herself had been so dazed she hadn't even realized that he was there. Would she have noticed Jasper, or cared if he were there? That night, as he thought about it, it had seemed like a waste of time. Jasper had wasted his time.

But he'd since revised his thinking. He'd never been in such an awful place—the walls, the odor, the putrescence, the children crying. Jasper had said, "Programs don't solve problems, people do. People caring about people." Maybe he hadn't been wasting his time. Jasper had been the better man.

One afternoon, back at the office, he had asked his secretary to try to phone Mimi Chance. He thought he'd check in to see if he could help them with anything. But she could locate no such person. The schools would have records of where the children had been sent. But he hadn't gotten their first names. He tried at Grant. The office had been in an uproar since the shooting. Nothing had been done. The only address they had for the James girl was her old one. No one had supplied them with a new one yet. And she hadn't been back to school since the shooting. He gave up.

The programs he had planned, the ones that he'd asked Jasper to look over, sat on his desk. He'd done nothing about them. He had no energy for them, and he wasn't sure they'd help anything anyway. What was really needed to make any headway were thousands of Hector Jaspers—younger, still-inspired, persistent. But that wasn't something the associate super could supply.

A class of older children came into the church sanctuary. While the kindergartners had filed in a few days ago in an orderly line, these children slouched and talked and shoved each other. They were in uniforms—the girls in their plaid skirts, the boys in ties and sweaters. But they were all at odd heights and sizes, the vagaries of adolescence. The teacher bustled in behind them and read off names. Reluctantly, they fell into a double line in front of the altar, facing the pews. Two girls objected to where they were assigned and muttered, "Bitch," under their breaths when the teacher told them to stand where she'd told them. Boys in the back row shared some private joke and stumbled out of line, laughing.

The teacher scolded them and demanded their attention. For three seconds all eyes were on her. As soon as she turned to the piano, disorder reigned again. She pounded a chord. A girl in the front row screeched and grabbed at her back. The boys behind her guffawed again. "He put this down my blouse," she yelled as the teacher stormed over.

His peace disturbed, Leo got up and left. No, he couldn't work in the field. He cared about children, but only in the abstract.

Once in his car, he lit a cigarette and drove toward the office, but he dreaded getting there. He knew what awaited him, and he had no heart for it.

He thought of the disgusting funeral home. Was it really as bad as he remembered or had it just been the rain that day, the strangeness of going to a funeral for someone he didn't even know? He doubled back and drove by the building. A chain gate blocked the front of the door and two front windows. What was there inside to steal? The curtain at one of the windows was torn. The light bulb over the front door had been broken off. Only jagged edges of the bulb remained.

He finished his cigarette and lit another. Yes. It was as he remembered. Only the stench was missing.

It was depressing. All of it. The intractable problems—death, his restlessness, the state of his soul. He cared about the church abstractly, from a distance, the same way he cared about the children. Some exposure to reality was reassuring, but not too much of it. Too much exposure made him depressed, made him dwell on his shortcomings.

Holding the cigarette in his teeth, squinting through the smoke, he turned the car around and headed for work. There would be no mourners at his funeral. But he didn't care to think about that. He just had to figure out how to get through the next fourteen months.

The answer slid easily into his mind. He'd go back to stressing test scores. That's what he'd been hired to do. Give the superintendent and the school board what they wanted, garner some praise and fine recommendations and move on. He'd had some thoughts about starting an educational software company in California.

The closest way to work was over the hill, past Grant. A group of students was hanging around out front, not far from a security guard in a yellow jacket, who stood on the steps, a walkie-talkie to his ear. Leo stopped and stared up at the old building. A frieze running above the school's name depicted a globe, a test tube, some open books, a telescope, an artist's palette. The sculptor had dealt in hope and inspiration. It almost seemed like a joke now. Ulysses S. Grant High School. A general, Leo thought, and chuckled. Damned successful one, too.

He idled the car and lit another cigarette. But President Grant had been tainted. A drunk, head of one of the most corrupt administrations in the history of the presidency, he had accomplished nothing to bring all the newly freed slaves into American society. Odd name for a school, particularly here.

An idea came to him. He pulled out into the traffic and started toward his office. Hector A. Jasper High School. A nod to the community in its time of grief. He would score points for sensitivity. All the other principals would be soothed and flattered. It would make his life a lot easier while he returned to his original agenda for the next fourteen months.

He drove on, congratulating himself for this stroke of genius. Now, while everyone was still so shocked and upset, he was sure he could get the name-change passed by the Board. Jasper himself would have loved it.

He stubbed out the cigarette and turned the corner. He'd gotten so morbid, sitting in that damned church. He hadn't been able to move or make a single decision. Suddenly he felt stronger, more in control than he'd felt in weeks. Things were looking up.

So here cometh
"Delphinium Blossoms"
To recognize excellence in writing
And bring it to the attention
Of the careful reader
Being a book of the heart
Wherein is an attempt to body forth
Ideas and ideals for the betterment
Of men, eke women
Who are preparing for life
By living. . . .

(In the manner of Elbert Hubbard,
        "White Hyacinths," 1907)